PLANES and PILOTS

THE MESSERSCHMITT
Me 109

Volume II
From 1942 to 1945

(From F to K and Post-war derivatives)

Dominique BREFFORT
André JOUINEAU
Translated from the French by Alan Mckay

HISTOIRE & COLLECTIONS

PRINCIPAL MILITARY EVENTS FROM 1942 TO 1945

1942

1 July: German troops commanded by von Manstein take Sebastopol.

10 July: British take over and stabilise the front at El Alamein.

28 July: Rostov taken by the Germans heading for the Volga.

4-9 August: von Paulus' offensive and invasion of the Caucasus.

18 August: Anglo-Canadian landing at Dieppe a failure.

20 August: Germans reach the Volga.

5 September: Rouen bombed by the Allies.

12 September: Street-fighting begins in Stalingrad.

13 September: Elista (Caucasus) captured.

23 September: Montgomery begins his offensive at El Alamein.

25 October: Allied troop transports leave for French North Africa.

4 November: Rommel begins to retreat.

8 November: Allies land in Morocco and Algeria. In Egypt, the British recapture Mersa Matruh.

8-9 November: Vichy troops resist the landings in French North Africa.

11 November: Germans invade unoccupied part of France.

12 November: German airborne troops land in Tunisia.

13-15 November: British re-capture Tobruk.

20 November: Benghazi captured by the British.

23 November: German VIth Army encircled at Stalingrad.

27 November: French fleet scuttled at Toulon.

9 December: Allied offensive in Tunisia fails.

12 December: Von Manstein's offensive to relieve Stalingrad fails.

13 December: Rommel evacuates El Agheila.

30 December: Germans evacuate the Trek line in the Caucasus.

1943

4 January: Italian position in the Fezzan captured by a column from Leclerc's army.

9 January: General Russian offensive in the direction of Stalingrad.

13-17 January: Russian offensive towards Rostov.

23-24 January: Montgomery takes Tripoli.

31 January: Von Paulus captured at Stalingrad.

2 February: German VIth Army capitulates at Stalingrad.

4 February: British 4th Army enters Tunisia.

8 February: Russians recapture Kursk.

10-11 February: Russians take Belgogrod.

17 February: Rommel victorious at Gafsa.

22 February: Rommel's troops begin to retreat.

8-28 March: Rennes and Rouen bombed by Allies.

15 March: Kharkov recaptured by von Manstein.

20 March: Montgomery attacks Mareth line.

10 April: Montgomery enters Sfax.

12 April: Sousse taken by Franco-American troops.

7 May: Tunis and Bizerte captured.

12 May: General Giraud enters Tunis.

17 May: Bordeaux bombed by Allies.

5 July: German industrial and economic centres bombed.

10 July: Anglo-Americans land in Sicily.

12 July: Syracuse captured.

14 July: Allied bombings in the Paris region.

19-22 July: Rome bombed for the first time. Palermo taken.

1 August: Romanian oil installations bombed by Allies.

5 August: Russians re-capture Orel and Belgorod.

11 August: Russians re-capture Kharkov.

23 August: Berlin bombed.

24 August: Rome declared an open city.

3 September: British land at Reggio di Calabria.

8 September: Italian Army surrenders unconditionally.

9 September: Americans land at Salerno; Tarento captured.

10 September: Rome occupied by Germans.

16 September: Nantes bombed. Russian offensive towards Kiev.

23-25 September: Poltava and Smolensk captured.

1 October: Naples taken by Americans.

5-6 October: Germans evacuate Corsica.

16-25 October: Russians cross the Dniepr.

5-6 November: Vatican bombed. Kiev falls.

25 November: French troops enter Naples.

10 December: French troops engaged for the first time in Italy.

24 December: Offensive on Kiev started again.

1944

3 January: General Juin's French Expeditionary Corps arrives in Italy.

5-25 January: Battle of Garigliano.

11-20 January: Russian offensive to relieve Leningrad.

22 January: Americans land at Anzio.

1 February: Casino offensive begins. Germans counter-attack at Anzio.

4 March: Russian offensive towards the Carpathians.

15-20 March Russians enter Bessarabia.

25 March: Brazil sends an Expeditionary Corps.

8 April: Soviets attack Crimea.

10 April: Odessa captured.

15 April: Tarnopol captured.

21 April: Paris bombed by Allies.

23-25 April: The *Milice* attacks the Vercors.

9 May: Sebastopol re-captured by Russians.

11 May: General offensive in Italy.

26-31 May: French cities bombed.

1-3 June: Coastal fortifications and ports in France bombed.

4 June: Rome captured.

6 June: Allies land in Normandy.

8 June: Bayeux captured.

10 June: Russians reach Leningrad.

16 June: Americans gain a foothold in the Cotentin (France).

23-24 June: General Soviet offensive and capture of Vitebsk.

28 June: British attack Caen.

3 July: Sienna captured by French expeditionary force.

7 July: Minsk captured by Russians.

15 July: Russians reach the Niemen.

28 July: Russians reach the Vistula in Poland. Coutances, Avranches and Granville captured.

3-5 August: Allies advance into Brittany.

7 August: General Patton's troops liberate Brittany.

15 August: Franco-American landings in Provence.

21 August: Toulon surrounded.

25 August: Paris liberated by the 2e DB.

28 August: Marseilles taken.

31 August: Russians reach Bucharest in Rumania.

1 September: Greece evacuated by Germans.

2-6 September: Northern parts of France liberated.

6-7 September: Holland invaded.

11 September: Allies reach and enter for the first time in Germany.

25 September: Arnhem landings fail. Allies fall back on Lower Rhine.

2 October: American offensive on Aachen. Siegfried line penetrated.

4 October: Riga captured by Soviets.

10 October: Russians reach the Baltic. British occupy Corinth and the Peloponnese.

18 October: Russians reach Czechoslovakia.

21 October: Aachen capitulates.

24 October: Russian troops in Yugoslavia.

20 November: French 1re Armée liberates Belfort, Pattons frees Metz.

23 November: 2nf French AD liberates Strasbourg.

4-12 November: Progressive liberation of Alsace.

16 December: Von Runstedt's general offensive in the Ardennes.

20 December: Bastogne besieged by Germans.

29 December: Germans attack in the area of Sarrebrouck, Saverne and Sarrebourg.

1945

5 January: Germans attack north and south of Strasbourg.

9 January: Germans counter-attack in the East.

12 January: Great Russian offensive launched by Koniev and Zhukov.

17-18 January: Warsaw liberated.

2 February: Colmar captured by French 1re Armée.

16 February: Budapest falls.

1-3 March: Danzig encircled.

6 March: Cologne occupied.

9 March: Patton enters Koblenz.

19 March: De Lattre's army takes Sarrelouis.

21-25 March: The Palatinate occupied.

28-30 March: Russians enter Austria and Slovakia.

3 April: Messerschmitt factories captured by Russians.

14-18 April: Kiel and Leipzig taken. Patton's advance halted by order of the Allies.

Nuremberg captured. Russians march on Dresden and Berlin.

24 April: Berlin encircled.

1-2 May: Berlin capitulates.

4 May: Leclerc's troops reach Berchtesgaden.

6 May: Prague liberated.

7 May: German army surrenders unconditionally at Reims.

8 May: Keitel ratifies the agreement.

MESSERSCHMITT 109 from *FRIEDRICH* to *KARL*

The story of the Messerschmitt 109 is intimately linked with the that of the Luftwaffe between 1939 and 1945 and they were, so to speak, one and the same, revealing the prevarication, the uncertainty and other difficulties which marked the period.

The Me 109 was the symbol of the apparently invincible might of the IIIrd Reich's air force at the beginning of WWII with the *'Dora'* and the *'Emil'* versions*; Willy Messerschmitt's little marvel was produced throughout the conflict, the last versions that came off the production lines no longer having much in common with their predecessors from during the Phoney War.

It must be said that the strategic situation had completely changed, the hunter of the early days had now become the prey. Indeed, at the time, it was fighting on an equal footing — at worst! — with its opposite numbers, but it did need, month after month, to be modified so that it could face new situations; the engineers often had to find emergency solutions to the new threats it was ill-equipped to deal with.

The fearsome single-seater of the early days, light and agile like a bird of prey, never had a true successor — the 209 and the 309 were tried and tested at length but finally not mass-produced — and was never redesigned thoroughly. It was produced in many different variants and improved on in many different ways with the result that its power was increased, and therefore also its weight, making it less and less manoeuvrable.

This change of direction was not surprising when one knows that one of the main aims of the Luftwaffe was to protect the Fatherland, endlessly attacked by more and more heavily armed Allied bombers which were therefore increasingly difficult to get at.

The various patching-up changes which the 109 underwent throughout its career (stronger armament, modified cockpit canopy for better pilot visibility, enlarged tail-wheel or tyres for better stability on take-off and touch-down) never brought a long-lasting solution to the problems but only emphasised them.

Despite increasingly unfavourable circumstances and the challenge to its supremacy from another legendary aircraft, the Focke-Wulf 190, the Me 109 never let anyone down, enabling a good number of its pilots to obtain a creditable number of kills.

Within these pages, we invite you to relive this historic, noisy, violent and sometimes heroic period; as in the first volume, the better part of the book is given over to colour profiles of the camouflage systems used by the later versions of the Bf 109 (F, G and K) for which there were many different variants, reflecting the period's troubled and difficult circumstances.

Finally, the users of the various other versions of what was no doubt Germany's most famous WWII fighter, have not been forgotten, the prize being given to its distant relative the Ha 1112 *'Buchon'*, the result of the unlikely marriage between a Gustav and a Rolls Royce engine, built a long time after the end of the fighting. Some of them still fly nowadays but often only to take part peacefully in films!

---

* The different versions of the Me 109 like other German planes were identified by a letter and therefore bore a name taken from the German phonetic alphabet in use at the time by the Luftwaffe: A for Anton, B for Bertha, C for Cäsar, D for Dora, E for Emil, F for Friedrich and G for Gustav, etc. The only anomaly was K for Karl instead of the 'Konrad' that the rules stipulated.

FIGHTER GROUP INSIGNIA

This is not an exhaustive list of the wing, group and squadron insignia (*Geschwader*, *Gruppe* and *Staffel*) which will be shown in Me109 Profiles from the first operations until April 1945

JG 1

1./JG 1

2./JG 1
(until April 1943)

2./JG 1

3./JG 1

III./JG 1

8./JG 1
(until April 1943)

IV./JG 1

12./JG 2

Stab/JG 3

1./JG 3

3./JG 3
(until September 1943)

I./JG 3

7./JG 3

III./JG 3
(variant)

4./JG 4

JG 5

2./JG 5

5./JG 5

II./JG 5

7. (Z)/JG 5

8./JG 5

10. (Z)/JG

14. (Jabo)/JG 5

JG 6

3./JG 11

5./JG 11

I./JG 20

3./JG 20

3./JG 21

JG 26
(variant)

2./JG26
(beginning
of the war)

5./JG 26

6./JG 26

10. (Jabo)/JG 26

9./JG 26

Erg. Staffel/JG

9./JG 26

4./JG 27

5./JG 27

6./JG 27

9./JG 27

IV./JG 27

1./JGr 50

II./JG 51
(beginning of the war)

5./JG 51

II./JG 51
(end of the war)

I./JG52

2./JG 52

4./JG 52

7./JG 52

9./JG 52

15. (Kroat)/JG 52

JG 53

10. (N)/JG 53

10. (Jabo)/JG 53

JG 53

Stab I./JG 53

1./JG 54

2./JG54

3./JG54

II./JG 54

7./JG 54
(and of the war)

IV./JG 54
(and of the war)

13./JG 54

Stab/JG 77

2./JG 77

10. (N)/JG 77

III./JG 77

9./JG 77

11. (N)/JG 2

1./JG 102

1./JGr 102

JG 300

JG 300
(variant)

I./JG 300

8./JG 300

I./JG 302

1./Aufkl. Gr. 122

FFS A/B 123

7./EJG 5

EJG Öst

Erg. Gr./JG 54

NJG Schule

Jabostaffel
Afrika

Hans von Hahn's
personal insignia

Günther Scholz's
personal insignia

Detlev Rohwer's
personal insignia

Karl Rammelt 's
personal insignia

Insignia
of the *Infanterie
Sturmabzeichen*

3° Gruppo
autonomo (*Regia
Aeronautica*)

23° Gruppo
(*Reggia
Aeronautica*)

GIGI TRE OSEI
150° Gruppo
(*Reggia
Aeronautica*)

7th Company,
Swiss Air Force

7

DIFFERENT TYPES OF Bf 109F

N.B. This plate is a corrected version of the one appearing in the first volume, page 76

F-0

F-0
DB601N powerplant. Modifications compared with the Me 109E: rounded engine cowling, oil radiator intake (under the nose) smaller, reduced tail surfaces, enlarged and rounded propeller boss, shorter VDM propeller blades, shorter wingspan, rounded wingtips added, wider but shallower underwing radiators, different flaps, rudder without bracing struts, MG 151/20 cannon.

F-1
Identical to the F-0 except for a rounded turbo-charger intake. Bracing struts under horizontal tail surfaces.
F-1/B fitted with an ETC pylon to carry an SC 250 250kg bomb.
F-1/B Trop: tropicalised fitted with a sand filter, modification carried out in the field not in the factory using Italian filters.

F-1

F-2/Z

F-2
Identical to the F-1 but with an MG 151/15 canon with a increased rate of fire. Rounded wheel wells (like the end-of-production F-1s). Horizontal tail surface bracing struts on the first machines only. Produced at the same time as the F-1
F-2/B: fitted with an ETC 250 pylon.
F-2 Trop: fitted with a sand filter and survival gear.
F-2/Z: (nick-named 'Ha Ha' by the pilots) fitted with the nitrous oxide GM-1 power boost system. Larger intakes for radiators and turbo-charger. Unlikely to have been produced in great numbers.

F-3
Identical to the F-1 but with a DB601E engine using B4 fuel (87 octane, compared with the previous 96). Probably fifteen or so produced.
F-4
Identical to the F-3 (DB601E powerplant and MG 151/20 canon with 150 shells only). Further protection for the pilot by increasing the surface of the head-rest armour. Bracing struts on the first models only.
F-4/B: fighter-bomber, with various ETC bomb pylons.

F-4

F-4 Trop

F-4 Trop: sand filter and survival equipment.
F-4/Z: fitted with the GM-1 power boost system. Larger intakes for radiators and turbo-charger. Larger diameter VDM propeller on certain machines.

Modifications for reconnaissance missions (often designated F-5 and F-6 by mistake) with vertical camera and underbelly opening, behind the cockpit.
— **F-4/R-2** (Rb 20/30 camera).
— **F-4/R-3** (Rb 50/30 camera).

F-4/R2

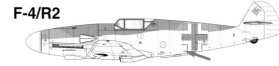

F-4/R8

F-4/R-4 (Rb 75/30) without radio (the space being occupied by the cameras), mast, antenna or cannon (perhaps also without the cowling-mounted machine guns in some cases).
F-4/R8: fitted either with an Rb 50/30 or an Rb 75/30 camera with radio equipment.
F-5: one model produced (summer 1941). High-altitude fighter version identical to the F-2 but using 100 octane fuel, a different propeller and MG 151/20 canon.
F-6: F-4 with reinforced armament, two extra machine guns in the wings. One machine thought to have been produced, but only with the engine-mounted guns fitted.

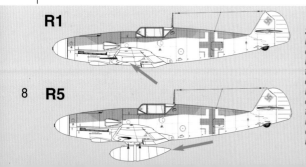

R1

R5

RUSTSÄTZE
Several conversion combinations (Rustsätze) could be mounted, but they did not change the designation of the machine.
R1: Two MG 151/20 cannon in underwing trays.
R5: underbelly 300-litre drop tank.
R6: ETC bomb launcher.

R6 (one SC 250 bomb)

R6 (four SC 50 bombs)

F for FRIEDRICH

The 'Friedrich' was without doubt the most handsome fighter of the long, prolific line of 109s. It was derived directly from the 'Emil' and was much more refined, slender, with round, harmonious lines which contrasted with the sharp outlines of the Emil, its predecessor.

This new silhouette represented the highest point of German fighters which nothing apparently could resist especially after their triumph during the Blitzkrieg, be it over the Channel, the North African Desert or the Russian steppes.

The evolution of the Friedrich goes back to the summer of 1940, almost at the time of the Battle of Britain, when the German engineers decided to make the Me 109 a bit younger by taking advantage of the fact that a new motor was available and could now equip Willy Messerschmitt's little fighter. This new engine improved performance generally but a few aerodynamic modifications went with it, like shortening the wings — at the same time giving them rounded tips and new flaps —, reducing propeller diameter, using a semi-retractable tailwheel and above all getting rid of the old-fashioned tail-plane braces which gave it a totally outmoded look.

It was this new structure which caused the tragic accidents which marred the beginning of the Friedrich's career. It seems that the engineers had underestimated the forces caused by the tail control surfaces and in particular, the heavy flutter at certain speeds which caused the loss of four machines at the beginning of 1941. The installation of reinforcements on the rearmost formers of the fuselage, at first on the outside, then on the inside of the cell cured these teething problems once and for all.

The Bf 109F was one of the principal reasons of the Luftwaffe's successes on the two totally different fronts, North Africa (Spring 1941) and the USSR (from 22 June of the same year). In order to be able to operate in the desert, the machine was 'tropicalised' ; this consisted of fitting a sand filter and installing survival equipment for forced landings.

The last version of the Friedrich, the F-4, which came off the production lines from June 1941 was both the most produced and the most successful. It was powered at last by the intended DB 610E, whose teething problems had prevented the earlier models receiving it. The plane's armament remained unchanged with a canon and two machine guns, all concentrated in the nose; the pilots' opinion about this concentration was divided. Some of them, like Walter Oesau refused to use the Friedrich because he missed the wing-mounted guns of the Emil, whereas others like Adolf Galland, insisted on the fact that this concentrated firepower simplified aiming for pilots who lacked their elders' experience.

If the Bf 109F did not have many variants, it was however used a lot as a flying test bed for some rather original, if not hare-brained, technical solutions: wider-spaced landing gear, tricycle undercarriage (for the Me 209 and 309), V-type tail surfaces, BMW radial engine, etc. The two most surprising modifications were without doubt the Bf 109H, which was built in limited numbers for high-altitude interception with a larger wingspan, and the Bf 109Z (Z for 'Zwilling', twin) which was two Friedrich fuselages coupled together. Note that a dozen or so F-4s were mounted on to the back of Ju-88s which had been transformed into flying bombs as part of the Mistel programme (or 'Beethoven Gerät'- Beethoven apparatus).

As far as exports were concerned, the Bf 109F was not very successful as, apart from the Luftwaffe, only Italy, Spain and Hungary bought any, and even then only a few of them.

THE FIRST VERSIONS of the Me 109F

Messerschmitt Bf 109 F-2 on the Eastern Front, winter 1941. All the upper surfaces have been daubed in white leaving the nationality markings and insignias visible.
(ECPA)

The Me 109F programme was launched at the beginning of 1940 at the *Bayerische Flugzeugwerke* and the *Wiener Neustäder Flugzeugwerke* (WNF), the first production machines of the first variant of this model coming out in the autumn of the same year.

The new plane had been thoroughly redesigned, compared with its predecessor it had more modern, aerodynamic lines which were not only elegant but effective, was powered by a Daimler-Benz DB 601 E which was more powerful than the Emil's 601N it was less heavily armed, the armament being concentrated in the nose (two cowling-mounted machine guns and one canon firing through the propeller boss), the wing mounted guns being discarded. As the new engine was still being perfected, it was replaced by the DB 601 N of the Bf 109 E-4/7, at first on the first ten pre-production machines (designated F-0) then on the F-1s and F-2s.

These two variants were distinguishable from preceding models by the air intake of the turbo-charger which was no longer rectangular but round. In spite of all this, with the same engines, the new models turned out to be far superior to their predecessors, further proof of their pedigree.

It was the famous Werner 'Vatti' Mölders, then a Major in the Stab./JG 51 who received the first production F-1 (W. Nr. 5628) aboard which he carried out the first operational sortie of the new model. This unit also had the unhappy privilege of losing the first 'Friedrich' when the 1./JG 51's Staffelkapitän's machine was lost over the British Isles on 11 November 1941.

But deliveries of the F-1 only really got under way in March 1941, once the accidents which had occurred with the pre-production machines had been investigated and reinforcements installed into the rear part of the fuselage. Because of these delays, the F-1s reached their units at the same time as the F-2s, whose production had been started in October 1940.

Originally only a limited number of F-2s - about a hundred - were to have been built, but in fact this model was produced in far greater numbers than its predecessor and over a longer period, production ending in August 1941.

Externally they were alike, the only difference being the canon installed in the F-2 which was reduced from 20 mm to 15 mm, the smaller calibre being compensated by a increased rate of fire.

Used by the most famous fighter units, the first two Bf 109F variants took part in the main Luftwaffe operations over the Libyan or Tunisian deserts, against the RAF in the West, and of course against the Soviet Union, after the launching of *Operation Barbarossa*.

The F-3 was the first variant to be fitted with the DB601E as originally planned; its armament was identical to that of the F-1 (one MG FF/M canon and two MG 17 machine guns).

Launched at the same time as the F-4, it was produced in very few numbers (at most fifteen machines) so much so that some people even doubt its existence. Indeed its existence is only borne out by a production plan dated October 1940 and two unit reports mentioning the loss of two machines of this type.

Before the appearance of the main and last variant, the F-4, a little less than 1 600 F-1s and F-2s came off the production lines in one year, from July 1940 to August 1941.

Me 109F-1 AND F-2 IN THE LUFTWAFFE

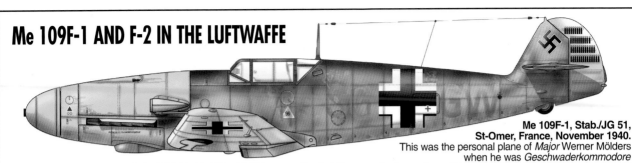

**Me 109F-1, Stab./JG 51,
St-Omer, France, November 1940.**
This was the personal plane of *Major* Werner Mölders
when he was *Geschwaderkommodore*
(Commander of a wing) of JG 51. *Vatti* (Pop) Mölders was the first German pilot to receive a Friedrich which he used for the first time in
October 1940. Camouflage, upper surfaces: RLM 74 and 75 (*Graugrün/Grauviolett*), lower surfaces: RLM 76 (*Lichtblau*), engine cowling
yellow (RLM 04 *Gelb*) a part of the factory code (*Stammkennzeichen*) can still be seen under the camouflage.

**Me 109F-2, 8./JG 26,
"Schlageter", based at Liegescourt
(France) in June 1941.** *Oberleutnant* Gustav Sprick's
Staffelkapitän (Flight Commander) plane. JG 26 was the first unit
to be equipped with the F-2 at the beginning of 1941 and was able to face up to the Spitfire Mk V
which came into service at about the same time. Camouflage, upper surfaces: RLM 74/75,
lower surfaces: RLM 76, engine cowling and tailfin yellow (RLM 04)

**Me 109F-2, 8./JG 52,
Mizil (Romania) June 1941.**
Pilot: *Obergefreiter* Friedrich Wachowiak.
JG 52 covered the southern front during Operation Barbarossa, the invasion of the Soviet Union.
Camouflage, upper surfaces: RLM 74/75, lower surfaces: RLM 76, only the lower part of the engine cowling was painted yellow (RLM 04)

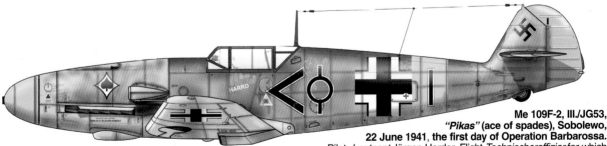

**Me 109F-2, III./JG53,
"Pikas" (ace of spades), Sobolewo,
22 June 1941, the first day of Operation Barbarossa.**
Pilot: *Leutnant* Jürgen Harder, Flight *Technischeroffizier* for which
the rank insignia has here an unusual form. Camouflage, upper surfaces: RLM 74, 75 and 02 (grau), lower surfaces: RLM 76. The yellow identification markings for the Eastern Front (RLM 04) were painted on the engine cowling (here the tone is slightly modified
by the extra paint), the rear of the fuselage and the wing tip lower surfaces. The TO's marking (a circle with vertical stripes) is a unusual variant.

Me 109F-2 IN THE LUFTWAFFE

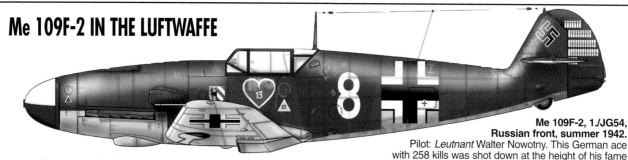

**Me 109F-2, 1./JG54,
Russian front, summer 1942.**
Pilot: *Leutnant* Walter Nowotny. This German ace
with 258 kills was shot down at the height of his fame
at the commands of another Messerschmitt fighter, the Me 262 *'Schwalbe'* (swallow), on 8 November 1944.Camouflage, upper surfaces:
RLM 70/71; lower surfaces: RLM 65 and identification markings, under the engine cowling and wingtips, yellow RLM 04. Partial fuselage stripe.

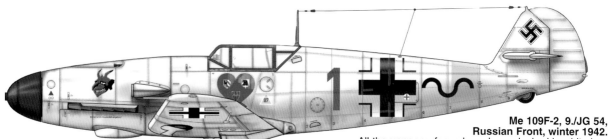

**Me 109F-2, 9./JG 54,
Russian Front, winter 1942.**
All the upper surfaces have been daubed in white lea-
ving the nationality markings and insignias visible. This temporary coat
did not last long, and it let the original camouflage through in parts. Inside the green heart are the three insignia of the groups
which made up the *Geschwader*, the insignia of the 9. Staffel being painted on the engine cowling.

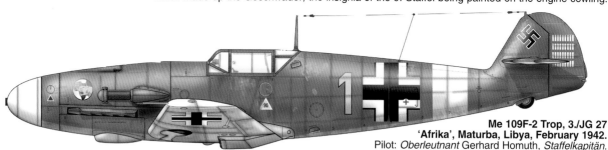

**Me 109F-2 Trop, 3./JG 27
'Afrika', Maturba, Libya, February 1942.**
Pilot: *Oberleutnant* Gerhard Homuth, *Staffelkapitän*.
This plane was fitted with a sand filter installed in front of the air intake
for the turbo-compressor and was camouflaged in the typical Luftwaffe colours for aircraft operating in North Africa, sand for the upper
surfaces (RLM 79) and light blue for the lower surfaces (RLM 78). The white markings for the Mediterranean theatre of operations
were painted in the usual places, boss, wing tips and fuselage stripe.

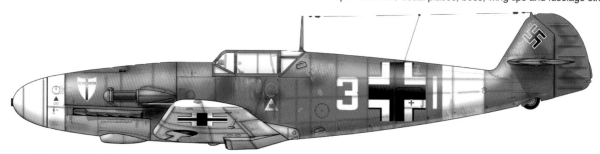

Me 109F-2, III./JG 27, Libya, Autumn 1942.
Note that the usual camouflage (RLM 79/78) has been completed with green marks (RLM 80)
in order to make it more effective and that a white band has been added to the front of the engine cowling.

Me 109F-2 IN THE LUFTWAFFE

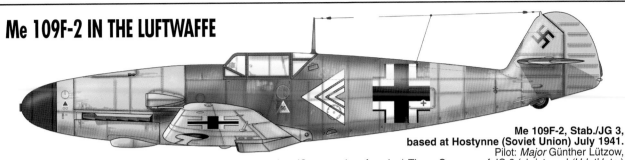

**Me 109F-2, Stab./JG 3,
based at Hostynne (Soviet Union) July 1941.**
Pilot: *Major* Günther Lützow,
Geschwaderkommodore (Commander of a wing) Three Gruppen of JG 3 (christened *'Udet' later*)
were part of *Luftflotte IV* which was operating in the south of the Soviet Union at the time of the invasion.
Camouflage, upper surfaces: RLM 74, 75 and 71; lower surfaces: RLM 76; identification markings in yellow (RLM 04).

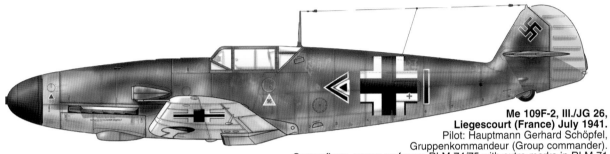

**Me 109F-2, III./JG 26,
Liegescourt (France) July 1941.**
Pilot: Hauptmann Gerhard Schöpfel,
Gruppenkommandeur (Group commander).
Camouflage, upper surfaces: RLM 74/75 with extra marks in RLM 71
lower surfaces: RLM 76; the underside of the engine cowling and the tailfin painted yellow (RLM 04)
are rapid identification markings standardised within this unit operating over the Channel and England.

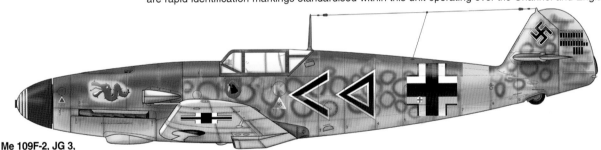

**Me 109F-2, JG 3,
'Udet', Russian Front, July 1941.**
This was one of the machines used by the famous Hans 'Hassi' von Hahn,
at the time *Geschwaderkommodore* (commander of a wing). The standard camouflage
for the upper surfaces, RLM 74/75, was complemented
by RLM 70 and 02 circles and marks; lower surfaces: RLM 76;
the yellow of the engine cowling has been softened to be less visible,
but the *'Tazelwurm'* has not been touched. The rank
markings and the propeller boss spiral
are quite unusual.

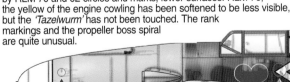

**Me 109F-2, Stab./JG 54,
Russian Front, October 1941.**
Pilot: *Major* Hannes Trautloft.
The camouflage used on the fighters in JG 54 *'Grünherz'* (Green heart)
were among the Luftwaffe's most original ones and were often adapted to the environment.
Here the camouflage upper surfaces are RLM 79/80 and the lower surfaces: RLM 78, and the identification markings yellow (RLM04)

Me 109F-2 IN THE LUFTWAFFE

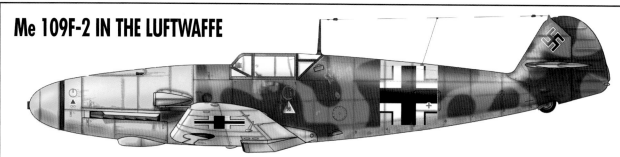

Me 109F-2, Stab./JG 54, Russian Front, Summer 1941
Camouflage, upper surfaces: RLM 79/80 (Sandgelb/Olivgrün); lower surfaces: RLM 78 (Hellblau)
Identification markings yellow (RLM 04).

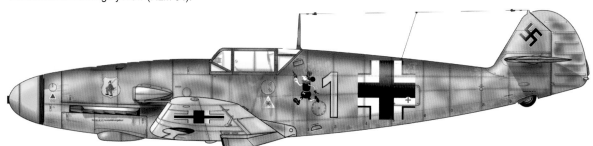

Me 109F-2, 4./JG 54, Russian Front, August 1941.
Pilot: *Oberleutnant* Hans Schmoller-Haldy, *Staffelkapitän* of the flight.
Camouflage, upper surfaces: RLM 74/75; lower surfaces:
RLM 76. Note that only the lower half of the fuselage stripe
has been painted.

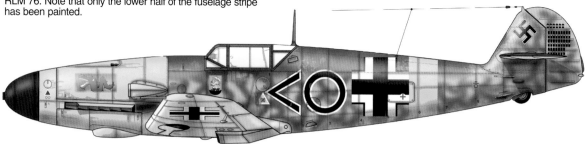

Me 109F-2, I./JG 3, based at Byelaya-Zerkov, Soviet Union, August 1941.
Pilot: *Leutnant* Detlev Rower, *Gruppentechnischeoffizier* (Group technical officer)
Camouflage, upper surfaces: RLM 74/75; lower surfaces: RLM 76
identification markings yellow (RLM 04). Note here again,
that the position of the *Tazelwurm* (I./JG 3's insignia)
on the cowling has not been covered over.

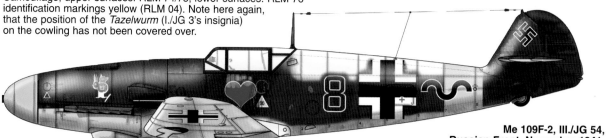

**Me 109F-2, III./JG 54,
Russian Front, November 1941.**
The camouflage for the upper surfaces is very classic: RLM 70/71,
(*Schwarzgrün* and *Dunkelgrün*) with the lower surfaces, pale blue
(RLM 65, *Hellblau*). White paint has been daubed on to part of the fuselage
identification markings yellow (RLM 04).

Me 109F-2 IN THE LUFTWAFFE

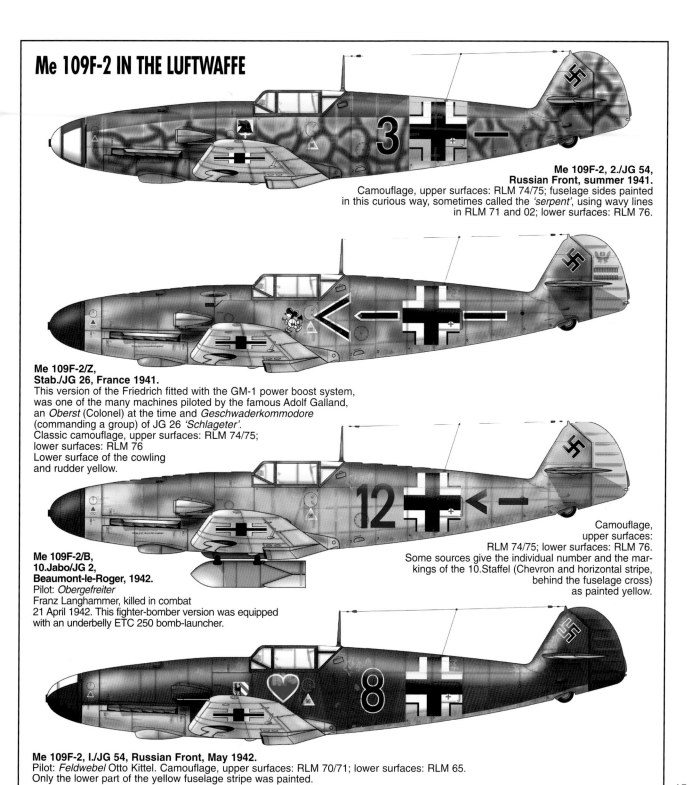

**Me 109F-2, 2./JG 54,
Russian Front, summer 1941.**
Camouflage, upper surfaces: RLM 74/75; fuselage sides painted
in this curious way, sometimes called the *'serpent'*, using wavy lines
in RLM 71 and 02; lower surfaces: RLM 76.

**Me 109F-2/Z,
Stab./JG 26, France 1941.**
This version of the Friedrich fitted with the GM-1 power boost system,
was one of the many machines piloted by the famous Adolf Galland,
an *Oberst* (Colonel) at the time and *Geschwaderkommodore*
(commanding a group) of JG 26 *'Schlageter'*.
Classic camouflage, upper surfaces: RLM 74/75;
lower surfaces: RLM 76
Lower surface of the cowling
and rudder yellow.

Camouflage,
upper surfaces:
RLM 74/75; lower surfaces: RLM 76.
Some sources give the individual number and the markings of the 10.Staffel (Chevron and horizontal stripe,
behind the fuselage cross)
as painted yellow.

**Me 109F-2/B,
10.Jabo/JG 2,
Beaumont-le-Roger, 1942.**
Pilot: *Obergefreiter*
Franz Langhammer, killed in combat
21 April 1942. This fighter-bomber version was equipped
with an underbelly ETC 250 bomb-launcher.

Me 109F-2, I./JG 54, Russian Front, May 1942.
Pilot: *Feldwebel* Otto Kittel. Camouflage, upper surfaces: RLM 70/71; lower surfaces: RLM 65.
Only the lower part of the yellow fuselage stripe was painted.

THE F-4, THE MOST HANDSOME of the Bf 109?

The F-4, which started arriving in the units a short time after the F-2, was the most numerous variant of the Friedrich, some authors adding that it was perhaps the most successful of the Bf 109s.

It was actually nothing but a Friedrich as it had been conceived from the outset, i.e. powered by a DB61E, like its fleeting predecessor the F-3, and armed with a 20 mm MG 151/20 canon. However, this weapon had its ammunition reduced to 150 shots only. The pilot's protection had been improved by the addition of armour plate, placed in the moving part of the canopy, which itself was bigger. One of the undoubted advantages of the new motor was that it ran on B-4 low-octane (87) fuel, which was much easier to produce than the 96-octane C-3 octane of the previous engines.

The enlarged turbo-charger air intake, like on all the Z variants using the power boost system, appeared in the course of production, whereas the armoured windshield was to be found more frequently on the F-4s than on the other variants, even though it was not standard production equipment. The self-sealing tanks were improved and the first machines still had braced tailplanes which were quickly replaced by internal bracing.

More than 1 800 (1841?) F-4s were produced from 1941 to 1943 and were used by almost all the fighter units of the time. Its role however on the Western front was minimal, especially as an interceptor, because of the arrival of the much more effective Fw 190As. The II./JG 26 was thus the only unit to use it during the winter of 1941-42 before moving on to the Fw 190 or the Bf 109G. On the other hand, as fighter-bombers, the F-4/Bs of the 10. (Jabo)/JG 2 at Beaumont-le-Roger and the 10. (Jabo)/JG 26 at Poix, two units specially created with this intention, were very

F-4 Tropicalised from the III./JG 27 destroyed by the RAF in September 1942. The sand filter on the air intake is a modification carried out in the field. *(IWM)*

successful on missions over south-east England and effectively harassed the port installations, the defence systems and Allied shipping operating in the Channel out of all proportion to the number of aircraft used.

Another hunting ground where this version of the Friedrich gave a good account of itself was in North Africa where the very famous Hans Joachim Marseille (3./JG 27) made a reputation for himself. Using as he did at least four F-4Z (tropical versions equipped with the GM1 supercharger) all coded '14 yellow', the 'Star' of Africa got his 100th kill on 18 June 1942, and on 1 September of the same year shot down 17 planes in one day!

In spite of the arrival of the 'Gustav', its successor, the 109F reigned supreme for a few more months in the Mediterranean theatre, until the appearance of the Spitfire Mk V and despite a lot of hitches with its canon caused by the climate. It was under these conditions that the reduction in armament (three guns) showed its limits, especially when attacking bombers; the Friedrich pilots had to shoot very accurately.

It is on the Eastern front that the F-4 was most successful, its performance and armament being absolutely devastating when faced with, it is true, totally inferior opposition. Werner Mölders, Geschwaderkommodore of the JG 51, a veteran of the Spanish Civil War, of the Blitzkrieg and of the Battle of Britain overtook the German WWI ace of aces, von Richtofen's score at the end of June 1941 and got his 101st kill two weeks later! There were many pilots who passed the 100th victory mark during this campaign, like Major Gordon Gollob of the JG 77, the tenth Expert (ace) to reach 100 kills with his F-4 (May 1942). At this time Russian fighter units (the VVS) were starting to get dangerous mainly because of the appearance of new and more modern machines. But the pilots who exceeded 200 kills did so aboard F-4s.

Because of its short career, squeezed between the Emil and the Gustav, the Bf 109F was not used abroad a lot. Spain received fifteen or so F-4s which were used by the *Escuadron Azul*, officially the 15. (Span.)/JG 51, until July 1943; the *Magyar Kiralyi Legiero* (the Hungarian air force) replaced its Reggiane 2000s with F-4s in one fighting unit, within the Luftwaffe on the Eastern front. Finally Italy was the third country to use F-4s and F-4/Bs from the beginning of 1943, in the *3° and 150° Gruppi Caccia Terrestre*.

Specifications of the Bf 109F-4

Type: Single-seat fighter.
Powerplant: One Daimler-Benz DB 605E liquid-cooled 12-cylinder inverted-Vee engine rated at 1 300bhp.

Dimensions
Wingspan: 9.92 m *Length:* 8.90 m
Height: 2.60 m
Wing area: 16.10m²
Weight (empty): 2 590kg
Weight (loaded): 3 117kg

Performance
Max. Speed: 624 kph at 6 500 m

Cruising Speed: 498kph at 4 950m.
Rate of Climb 22.1 m/s.
Max. Range: 850kms or 1h 24 mins with extra tank.

Armament
One MG 151/20 20 mm canon with 150 rounds firing through the propeller boss.

Two MG 17 7.92-mm machine guns with 500rpg, mounted on a light alloy frame over the engine and firing through the propeller arc.

Me 109F-4 IN THE LUFTWAFFE

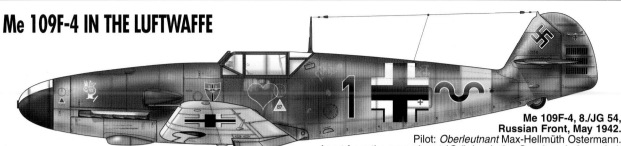

Me 109F-4, 8./JG 54,
Russian Front, May 1942.
Pilot: *Oberleutnant* Max-Hellmüth Ostermann.
Apart from the green heart (*Grünherz*), the *Geschwader*'s symbol,
the aircraft also bears the shield of the first *Gruppe* (under the windshield) and of the second *Staffel* (on the bonnet)
of JG 21 which became 8./JG 54 in July 1940. Camouflage, upper surfaces: RLM 70/71, lower surfaces: RLM 65.
Yellow Eastern Front identification marks (RLM 04).

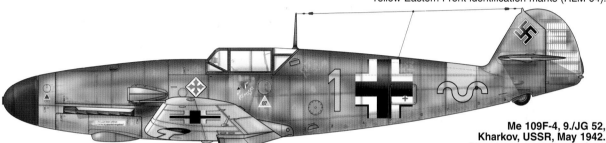

Me 109F-4, 9./JG 52,
Kharkov, USSR, May 1942.
Pilot: *Leutnant* Hermann Graf,
Staffelkapitän at the time, and who survived the war with more than 200 victories
Camouflage, upper surfaces: RLM 74/75, lower surfaces: RLM 76, identification marks yellow (RLM 04),
under the engine cowling, the wing tips and the fuselage stripe.

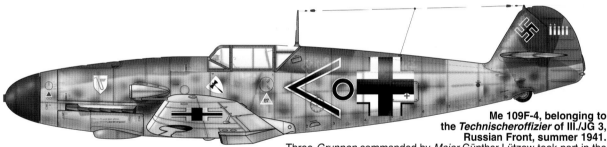

Me 109F-4, belonging to
the *Technischeroffizier* of III./JG 3,
Russian Front, summer 1941.
Three *Gruppen* commanded by *Major* Günther Lützow took part in the
invasion of Russia, within *Luftflotte IV*, from June 22, 1941 onwards. Camouflage, upper surfaces: RLM 74 and 75 with extra green
marks (RLM 71) on the fuselage sides, lower surfaces: RLM 76, yellow identification marks (RLM 04).

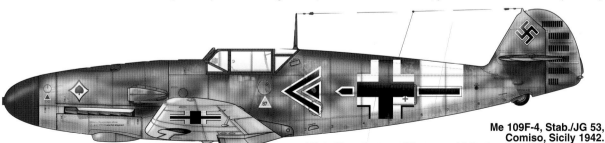

Me 109F-4, Stab./JG 53,
Comiso, Sicily 1942.
Pilot: *Oberstleutnant* Günter von Maltzahn, *Geschwaderkommore*
(Commanding a wing) witness the double chevron and the horizontal stripes on either side of the fuselage *Balkenkreuz*.
At the time, his unit was engaged in the attacks against Malta. Camouflage, upper surfaces: RLM 74 and 75 with extra green
(RLM 71) marks, lower surfaces: RLM 76. Note that apart from the white fuselage stripe which was characteristic of the
Mediterranean theatre of operations, the underside of the engine cowling has been painted yellow and the propeller boss blue.

17

Me 109F-4 IN THE LUFTWAFFE

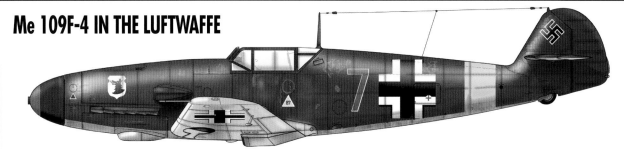

Me 109F-4, 8./JG 77, *Herzas* (Ace of Hearts), Russian Front, summer 1941.
Camouflage, upper surfaces: RLM 70/71, lower surfaces: RLM 76. The Eastern Front identification marks are limited to the yellow (RLM 04) fuselage band. The tip of the propeller boss is red, the colour of the 8. Staffel.

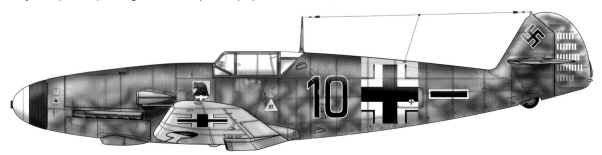

Me 109F-4, 5./JG 54, Ovischtchi, USSR, August 1941.
Pilot: *Oberleutnant* Hubert Mütherich, *Staffelkapitän*. Camouflage, upper surfaces: RLM 74/75, lower surfaces: RLM 76; yellow identification marks (RLM 04).

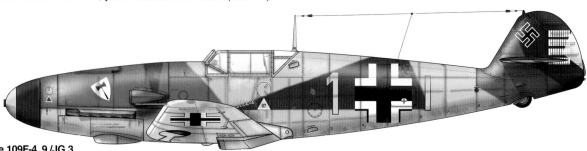

Me 109F-4, 9./JG 3,
Poland, July 1941.
Pilot: *Oberleutnant* Viktor Bauer.
This plane has a very unusual camouflage, made of large angular grey marks (RLM 74 and 76) and green (RLM 71) with the lower surfaces in classic pale grey (RLM 76). Yellow identification marks were limited to the fuselage stripe (RLM 04).

Me 109F-4, I./JG 52,
Russian Front, summer 1941.
Pilot: *Oberleutnant* Karl-Heinz Leesman. Camouflage, upper surfaces: RLM 74/75, lower surfaces: RLM 76; yellow identification markings (RLM 04) on the engine cowling, the tail and the wing tips. Note the unusual place of the *I. Gruppe*'s insignia behind the *Balkenkreuz* and the absence of the fuselage yellow stripe.

Me 109F-4 IN THE LUFTWAFFE

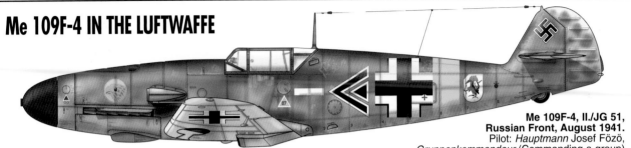

**Me 109F-4, II./JG 51,
Russian Front, August 1941.**
Pilot: *Hauptmann* Josef Fözö,
Gruppenkommandeur (Commanding a group)
Camouflage, upper surfaces: RLM 74/75, lower surfaces: RLM 76, yellow identification marks (RLM 04). The position
of the II./JG 52's insignia, behind the fuselage stripe, if unusual, was nevertheless common in this unit.

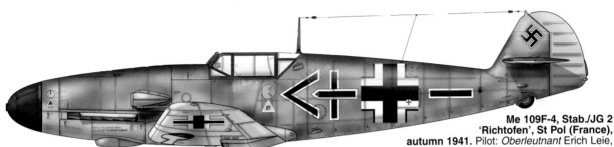

**Me 109F-4, Stab./JG 2
'Richtofen', St Pol (France),
autumn 1941.** Pilot: *Oberleutnant* Erich Leie,
Geschwaderadjudant (Adjutant for the wing). With the invasion
of the USSR, from June 1941, only two Jagdgeschwader (JG2 and JG 26)
operated in the West, over the Channel and England, within Luftflotte III. Camouflage, upper surfaces: RLM 74/75, lower surfaces:
RLM 76.Note the unusual rank markings, as well as the underside of the engine cowling and the tail painted yellow (RLM 04).

**Me 109F-4, II./JG 3,
Chatalowka, USSR, September 1941.**
Pilot: *Hauptmann* Gordon Gollob. Camouflage, upper surfaces:
RLM 74/75, lower surfaces: RLM 76, yellow identification markings
RLM 04). The tail painted grey (RLM 76) and dark green (RLM 71) bears the pilot's tally of kills. (He was *Kommandeur* at the time).
Gollob got his 100th kill on 20 May 1942, becoming the tenth Luftwaffe pilot to reach this symbolic figure.

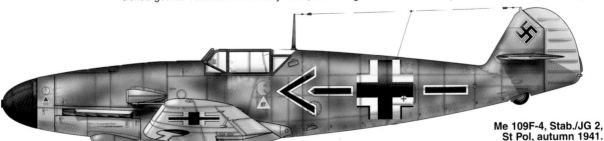

**Me 109F-4, Stab./JG 2,
St Pol, autumn 1941.**
Pilot: *Major* Walter Oesau, *Geschwaderkommodore*.
A impressive pilot and tactician, Oesau had trouble getting used
to the Friedrich, missing the additional firepower from the wing mounted guns on the Emil.
Camouflage, upper surfaces: RLM 74/75, lower surfaces: RLM 76, yellow lower engine cowling surface and tail (RLM 04).

Me 109F-4 IN THE LUFTWAFFE

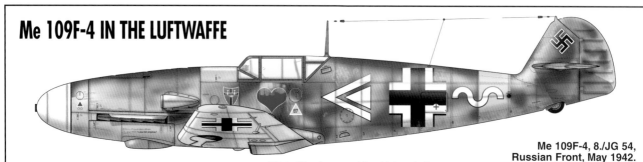

**Me 109F-4, 8./JG 54,
Russian Front, May 1942.**
Pilot: *Oberleutnant* Max-Helmuth Ostermann, *Staffelkapitän* (Flight commander)
Camouflage, upper surfaces: RLM 70/71, with extra greenish-grey marks (RLM 02) on the sides; lower surfaces: RLM 76. Yellow
identification markings (RLM 04). The totally white double chevron rank marking was rather unusual.

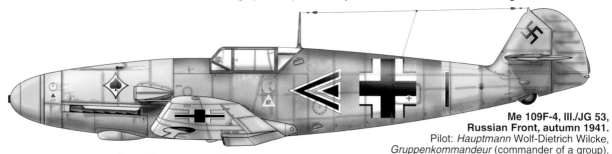

**Me 109F-4, III./JG 53,
Russian Front, autumn 1941.**
Pilot: *Hauptmann* Wolf-Dietrich Wilcke,
Gruppenkommandeur (commander of a group).
Camouflage, upper surfaces: RLM 74/75, lower surfaces: RLM 76, yellow identification markings (RLM 04).

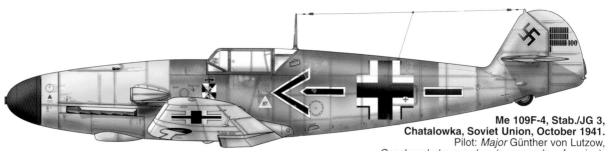

**Me 109F-4, Stab./JG 3,
Chatalowka, Soviet Union, October 1941.**
Pilot: *Major* Günther von Lutzow,
Geschwaderkommodore (commander of a wing).
Camouflage, upper surfaces: RLM 74/75, lower surfaces: RLM 76, yellow identification markings (RLM 04).

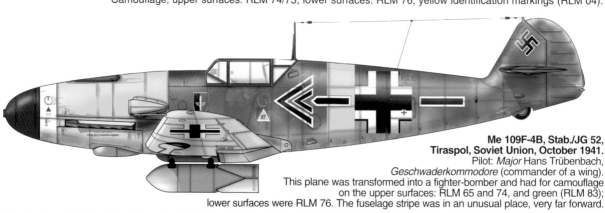

**Me 109F-4B, Stab./JG 52,
Tiraspol, Soviet Union, October 1941.**
Pilot: *Major* Hans Trübenbach,
Geschwaderkommodore (commander of a wing).
This plane was transformed into a fighter-bomber and had for camouflage
on the upper surfaces: RLM 65 and 74, and green (RLM 83);
lower surfaces were RLM 76. The fuselage stripe was in an unusual place, very far forward.

20

Me 109F-4 IN THE LUFTWAFFE

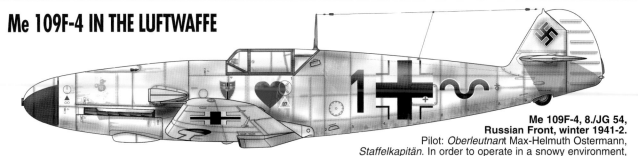

**Me 109F-4, 8./JG 54,
Russian Front, winter 1941-2.**
Pilot: *Oberleutnant* Max-Helmuth Ostermann,
Staffelkapitän. In order to operate in a snowy environment,
all the upper surfaces of the aircraft, as well as the sides, were daubed with white paint,
only the unit markings and the insignia were kept. Lower surfaces: RLM 76.

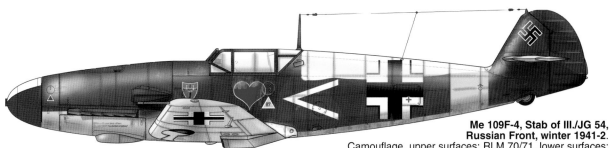

**Me 109F-4, Stab of III./JG 54,
Russian Front, winter 1941-2.**
Camouflage, upper surfaces: RLM 70/71, lower surfaces:
RLM 76, yellow identification markings (RLM 04).
The top rear surface of the fuselage and no doubt of the wings as well,
were daubed with white paint. The *Gruppenadjudant's* marking has an unusual shape.

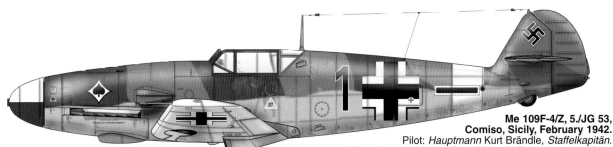

**Me 109F-4/Z, 5./JG 53,
Comiso, Sicily, February 1942.**
Pilot: *Hauptmann* Kurt Brändle, *Staffelkapitän*.
The plane was camouflaged in a similar way to machines
in North Africa, made of large sand-coloured (RLM 80) and green (RLM 71) marks with lower surfaces in RLM 76,
the limit between the two tones being at mid-fuselage level.

**Me 109F-4B, 10 (Jabo)./JG 2,
France, March 1942.**
Pilot: *Hauptmann* Frank Liesenthal.

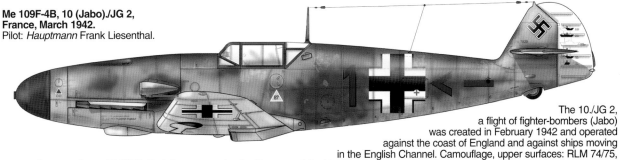

The 10./JG 2,
a flight of fighter-bombers (Jabo)
was created in February 1942 and operated
against the coast of England and against ships moving
in the English Channel. Camouflage, upper surfaces: RLM 74/75,
lower surfaces: RLM 76. Certain sources give the figures and the identification markings as being yellow with the flight insignia painted
on the engine cowling. The victory markings were painted on the tail and represented the ships sunk or damaged by the pilot.

Me 109F-4 IN THE LUFTWAFFE

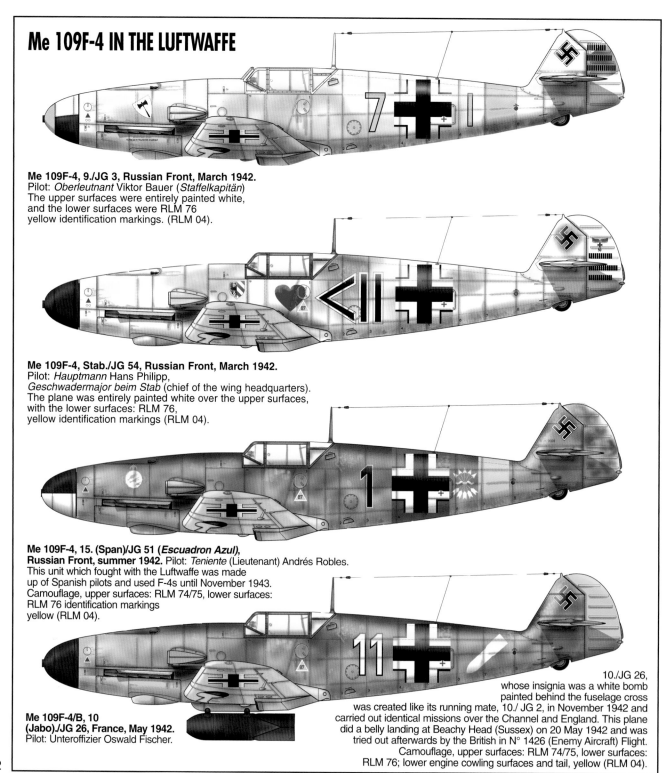

Me 109F-4, 9./JG 3, Russian Front, March 1942.
Pilot: *Oberleutnant* Viktor Bauer (*Staffelkapitän*)
The upper surfaces were entirely painted white,
and the lower surfaces were RLM 76
yellow identification markings. (RLM 04).

Me 109F-4, Stab./JG 54, Russian Front, March 1942.
Pilot: *Hauptmann* Hans Philipp,
Geschwadermajor beim Stab (chief of the wing headquarters).
The plane was entirely painted white over the upper surfaces,
with the lower surfaces: RLM 76,
yellow identification markings (RLM 04).

**Me 109F-4, 15. (Span)/JG 51 (*Escuadron Azul*),
Russian Front, summer 1942.** Pilot: *Teniente* (Lieutenant) Andrés Robles.
This unit which fought with the Luftwaffe was made
up of Spanish pilots and used F-4s until November 1943.
Camouflage, upper surfaces: RLM 74/75, lower surfaces:
RLM 76 identification markings
yellow (RLM 04).

**Me 109F-4/B, 10
(Jabo)./JG 26, France, May 1942.**
Pilot: Unteroffizier Oswald Fischer.

10./JG 26,
whose insignia was a white bomb
painted behind the fuselage cross
was created like its running mate, 10./ JG 2, in November 1942 and
carried out identical missions over the Channel and England. This plane
did a belly landing at Beachy Head (Sussex) on 20 May 1942 and was
tried out afterwards by the British in N° 1426 (Enemy Aircraft) Flight.
Camouflage, upper surfaces: RLM 74/75, lower surfaces:
RLM 76; lower engine cowling surfaces and tail, yellow (RLM 04).

Me 109F-4 IN THE LUFTWAFFE

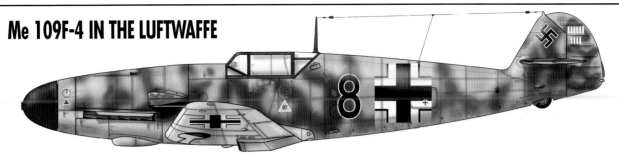

Me 109F-4, 2./JG 54, Russian Front, summer 1942.
Pilot: *Oberfeldwebel* Fritz Tegtmeier.
Camouflage, upper surfaces: RLM 70, 71 and 76,
lower surfaces: RLM 76; yellow identification markings (RLM 04).

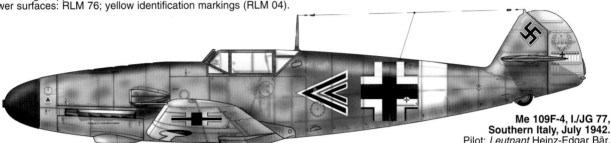

Me 109F-4, I./JG 77,
Southern Italy, July 1942.
Pilot: *Leutnant* Heinz-Edgar Bär,
Gruppenkommandeur, whose tally of kills, already more than 100,
was painted on the tail with his decorations (Iron Cross). Some weeks later, this unit was transferred to North Africa.
Camouflage, upper surfaces: RLM 74/75, lower surfaces: RLM 76; white Mediterranean theatre identification stripe.

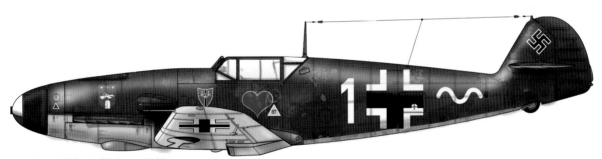

Me 109F-4, 7./JG 54, Finland, 1942.
Camouflage, upper surfaces: RLM 70/71, lower surfaces: RLM 65
identification markings yellow (RLM 04).

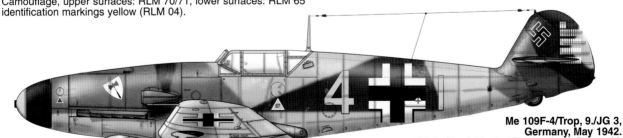

Me 109F-4/Trop, 9./JG 3,
Germany, May 1942.
Pilot: *Oberfeldwebel* Eberhard von Boremski.
This plane had unusual camouflage made up of large angular green
(RLM 71) and grey (RLM 02) marks on a pale grey background (RLM 76) which was also used for the underside. However,
as I and III./JG 3 had received a delivery of F-4 Trop destined for North Africa, and it is possible that this particular camouflage
was only an adaptation of the original North African scheme, the colour which was thought to have been identified on the black and
white photos as being grey (RLM 02) was in fact only sand (RLM 79).

23

Me 109F-4 IN THE LUFTWAFFE

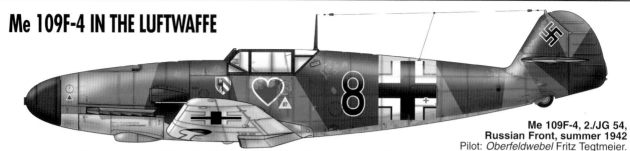

**Me 109F-4, 2./JG 54,
Russian Front, summer 1942**
Pilot: *Oberfeldwebel* Fritz Tegtmeier.
As was characteristic of the *Grünherz*, this plane has been camouflaged in one of the many different and original ways
and adapted to the environment. It had large angular stripes of green (RLM 71), greenish grey (RLM 02) and brown (RLM 79)
on the upper surfaces and the sides, the underside being blue-grey (RLM 76) with yellow identification markings (RLM 04).

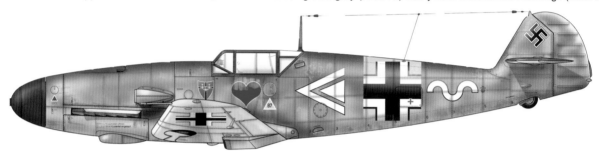

Me 109F-4, III./JG 54, Russian Front, summer 1942
Pilot: *Hauptmann* Reinhard Seiler, *Gruppenkommandeur* (commanding the third group).
Camouflage, upper surfaces: RLM 74/75, lower surfaces: RLM 76, yellow identification marks (RLM 04).

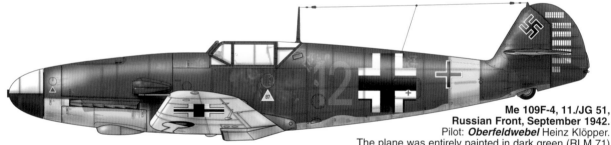

**Me 109F-4, 11./JG 51,
Russian Front, September 1942.**
Pilot: *Oberfeldwebel* Heinz Klöpper.
The plane was entirely painted in dark green (RLM 71)
on the upper surfaces, with RLM 65 underneath. Yellow identification markings (RLM 04).
The mark of IV. Gruppe (the cross) has been painted in an unusual place.

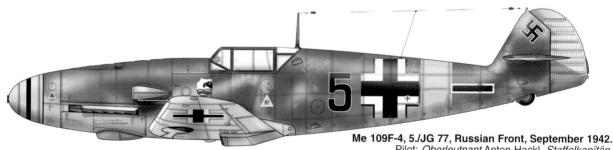

Me 109F-4, 5./JG 77, Russian Front, September 1942.
Pilot: *Oberleutnant* Anton Hackl, *Staffelkapîtän.*
Camouflage, upper surfaces: RLM 74/75, lower surfaces: RLM 76,
Yellow identification markings (RLM 04).

Me 109F-4 IN THE LUFTWAFFE

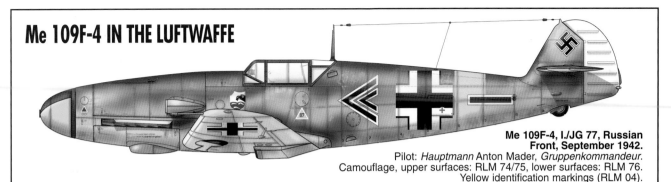

**Me 109F-4, I./JG 77, Russian
Front, September 1942.**
Pilot: *Hauptmann* Anton Mader, *Gruppenkommandeur*.
Camouflage, upper surfaces: RLM 74/75, lower surfaces: RLM 76.
Yellow identification markings (RLM 04).

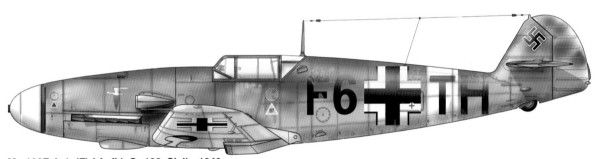

**Me 109F-4, III./JG 54,
Russian Front, winter 1942.**
This is one of the best-known of the Friedrichs,
with its original camouflage, upper surfaces: green (RLM 70/71)
and lower surfaces blue grey (RLM 76) partly daubed with white paint.
Yellow identification markings (RLM 04).

Me 109F-4, 1. (F)./ Aufkl. Gr 122, Sicily, 1942.
Fernkundungstaffeln were long-range reconnaissance
flights which used camera equipped F-4/Rs, often designated erroneously F-5 or F-6.
As opposed to the fighters the reconnaissance planes were identified
by four letter and figure fuselage codes.
Camouflage, upper surfaces: RLM 74/75, lower surfaces:
RLM 76. Mediterranean theatre white identification stripe.

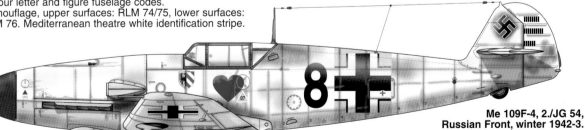

**Me 109F-4, 2./JG 54,
Russian Front, winter 1942-3.**
Pilot: *Oberfeldwebel* Fritz Tegtmeier.
This is the same machine as on the previous page
but the upper surface camouflage has been daubed white
without touching the underside (RLM 75) and the yellow identification markings (RLM 04).

THE Me 109F-4 IN FOREIGN COLOURS

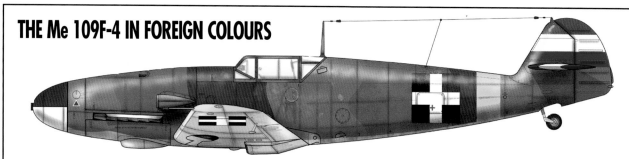

Me 109F-4, *Magyar Kiralyi Legiero* (Royal Hungarian air force), end of 1942.
Hungary received its first F-4s in October 1942 to replace its
Reggiane Re 2000s and used them on the Russian Front.
This aircraft bears an experimental camouflage
scheme which in the end was not used.

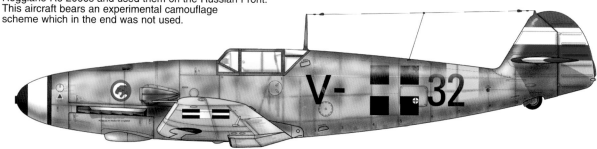

**Me F-4/B, 5/1 Squadron, the 'Red Pumas'
of the Hungarian Air Force. Eastern
Front, February 1943.**
The nationality markings on the fuselage
had no white. Camouflage, upper surfaces:
RLM 74/75, lower surfaces: RLM76.

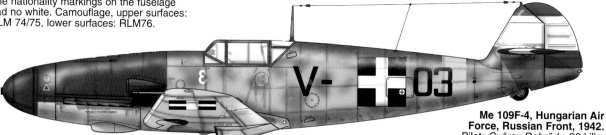

**Me 109F-4, Hungarian Air
Force, Russian Front, 1942.**
Pilot: *György Debrödy*, 26 kills.
Note that the engine cowling was partly painted dark green (RLM 71)
and that the flag painted on the tail consists of stripes of unequal widths.
Camouflage, upper surfaces: RLM 74/75, lower surfaces: RLM76.

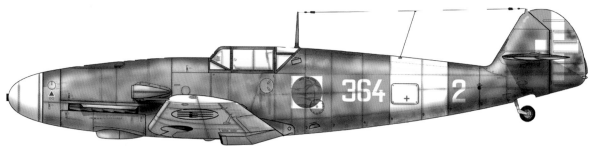

**Me 109F-4, 364a *Squadriglia*, *150° Gruppo Caccia Terrestre* (GCT)
of the *Regia Aeronautica* (Italian Air Force), Libya, 1943.**
The Italian Air Force received its first F-4s at the beginning of 1943 which made up two units (*3°* and *150° GCT*)
Camouflage, upper surfaces: RLM 74/75, lower surfaces: RLM 76.

Me 109F-4 TROP IN THE LUFTWAFFE

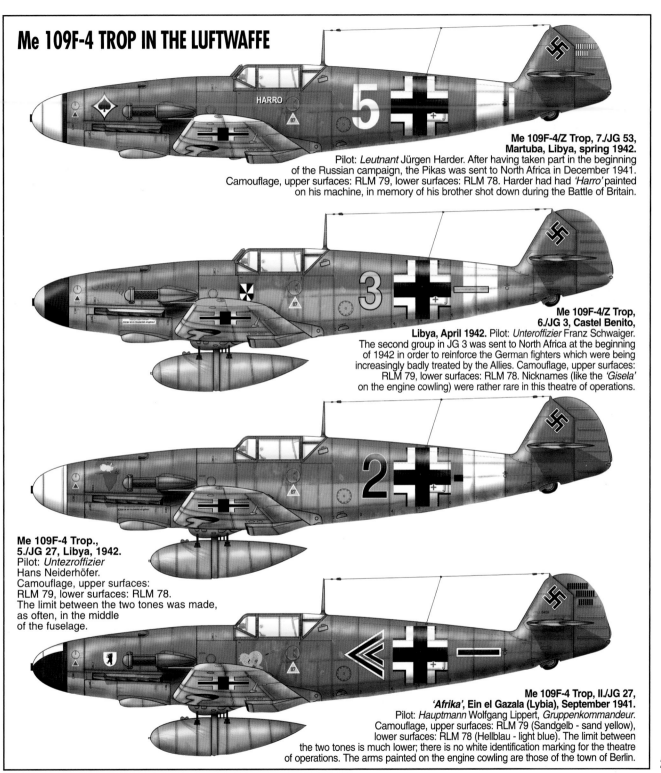

**Me 109F-4/Z Trop, 7./JG 53,
Martuba, Libya, spring 1942.**
Pilot: *Leutnant* Jürgen Harder. After having taken part in the beginning
of the Russian campaign, the Pikas was sent to North Africa in December 1941.
Camouflage, upper surfaces: RLM 79, lower surfaces: RLM 78. Harder had had *'Harro'* painted
on his machine, in memory of his brother shot down during the Battle of Britain.

**Me 109F-4/Z Trop,
6./JG 3, Castel Benito,
Libya, April 1942.** Pilot: *Unteroffizier* Franz Schwaiger.
The second group in JG 3 was sent to North Africa at the beginning
of 1942 in order to reinforce the German fighters which were being
increasingly badly treated by the Allies. Camouflage, upper surfaces:
RLM 79, lower surfaces: RLM 78. Nicknames (like the *'Gisela'*
on the engine cowling) were rather rare in this theatre of operations.

**Me 109F-4 Trop.,
5./JG 27, Libya, 1942.**
Pilot: *Untezroffizier*
Hans Neiderhöfer.
Camouflage, upper surfaces:
RLM 79, lower surfaces: RLM 78.
The limit between the two tones was made,
as often, in the middle
of the fuselage.

**Me 109F-4 Trop, II./JG 27,
'Afrika', Ein el Gazala (Lybia), September 1941.**
Pilot: *Hauptmann* Wolfgang Lippert, *Gruppenkommandeur*.
Camouflage, upper surfaces: RLM 79 (Sandgelb - sand yellow),
lower surfaces: RLM 78 (Hellblau - light blue). The limit between
the two tones is much lower; there is no white identification marking for the theatre
of operations. The arms painted on the engine cowling are those of the town of Berlin.

27

Me 109F-4 TROP IN THE LUFTWAFFE

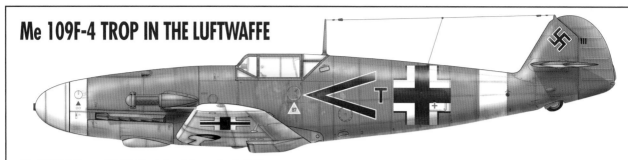

Me 109F-4 Trop, JG 27, Martuba, Libya, April 1942.
Pilot: *Oberleutnant* Rudolf Sinner, *Gruppentechnischeroffizier.*
Camouflage, upper surfaces: RLM 79, lower surfaces: RLM 78.

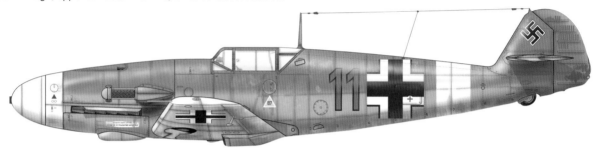

Me 109F-4 Trop, 2./JG 27, North Africa, June 1942.
Pilot: *Leutnant* Friedrich Körner.
Camouflage, upper surfaces: RLM 79, lower surfaces: RLM78.

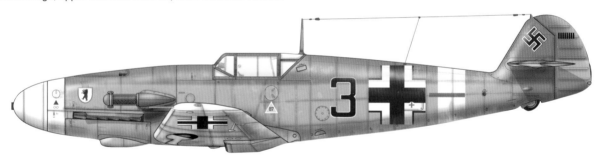

Me 109F-4 Trop, 6./JG 3, North Africa, spring 1942.
Pilot: *Unteroffizier* Franz Schwaiger
Camouflage, upper surfaces: RLM 79,
lower surfaces: RLM78.

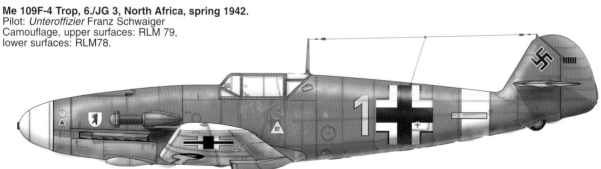

Me 109F-4, 6./JG 3, Tmimi, Libya, June 1942.
Pilot: *Oberleutnant* Rudolf Sinner
Camouflage, upper surfaces: RLM 79, lower surfaces: RLM78.

Me 109F-4 TROP IN THE LUFTWAFFE

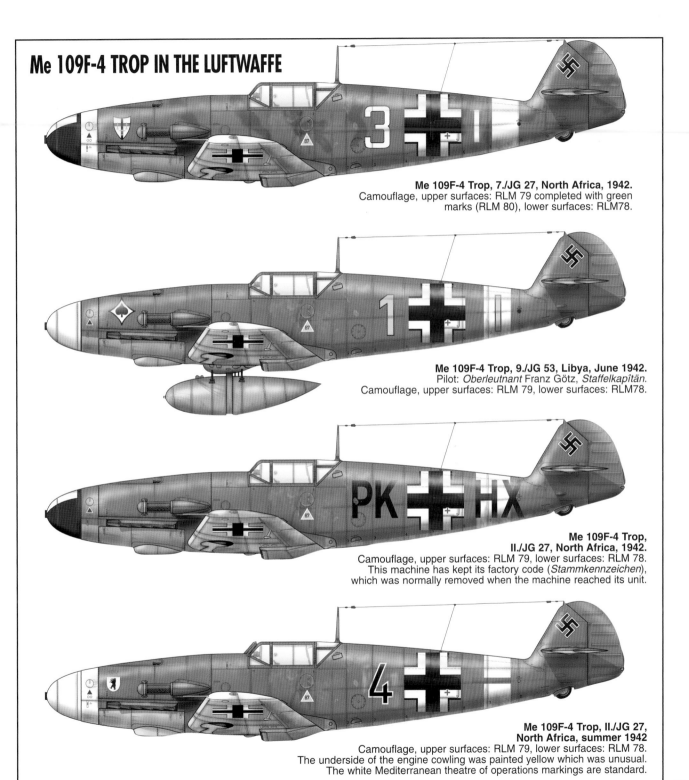

Me 109F-4 Trop, 7./JG 27, North Africa, 1942.
Camouflage, upper surfaces: RLM 79 completed with green
marks (RLM 80), lower surfaces: RLM78.

Me 109F-4 Trop, 9./JG 53, Libya, June 1942.
Pilot: *Oberleutnant* Franz Götz, *Staffelkapîtän.*
Camouflage, upper surfaces: RLM 79, lower surfaces: RLM78.

Me 109F-4 Trop,
II./JG 27, North Africa, 1942.
Camouflage, upper surfaces: RLM 79, lower surfaces: RLM 78.
This machine has kept its factory code (*Stammkennzeichen*),
which was normally removed when the machine reached its unit.

Me 109F-4 Trop, II./JG 27,
North Africa, summer 1942
Camouflage, upper surfaces: RLM 79, lower surfaces: RLM 78.
The underside of the engine cowling was painted yellow which was unusual.
The white Mediterranean theatre of operations markings are standard.

Me 109F-4 TROP IN THE LUFTWAFFE

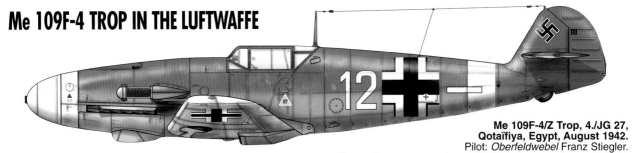

**Me 109F-4/Z Trop, 4./JG 27,
Qotaïfiya, Egypt, August 1942.**
Pilot: *Oberfeldwebel* Franz Stiegler.
Camouflage, upper surfaces: RLM 79, lower surfaces: RLM78.

**Me 109F-4 Trop, III./JG 27,
North Africa, September 1942.**
This machine was shot down by the RAF on 1 September 1942.
Camouflage, upper surfaces: RLM 79, lower surfaces: RLM78.

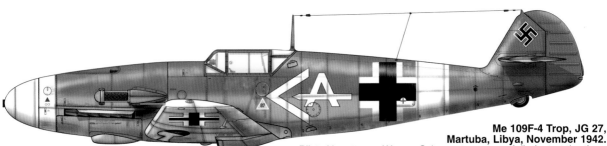

**Me 109F-4 Trop, JG 27,
Martuba, Libya, November 1942.**
Pilot: *Hauptmann* Werner Schroer, temporary Adjudant at the time,
which explains why there was an unusual marking behind the chevron, where an 'A' complements
the normal horizontal stripe. Camouflage, upper surfaces: RLM 79, lower surfaces: RLM78.

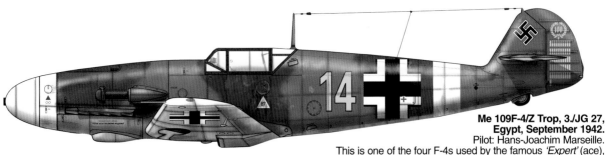

**Me 109F-4/Z Trop, 3./JG 27,
Egypt, September 1942.**
Pilot: Hans-Joachim Marseille.
This is one of the four F-4s used by the famous *'Expert'* (ace),
nick-named the *'Star of Africa'*, who got practically all his kills over the desert
and who had been made Staffelkapitän of 3./ JG 27 in June 1942. Like all his other planes, this one was coded '14 Yellow'
Camouflage, upper surfaces: RLM 79 with large green blotches (RLM 80), lower surfaces: RLM78.

THE VARIANTS of the Bf 109 F

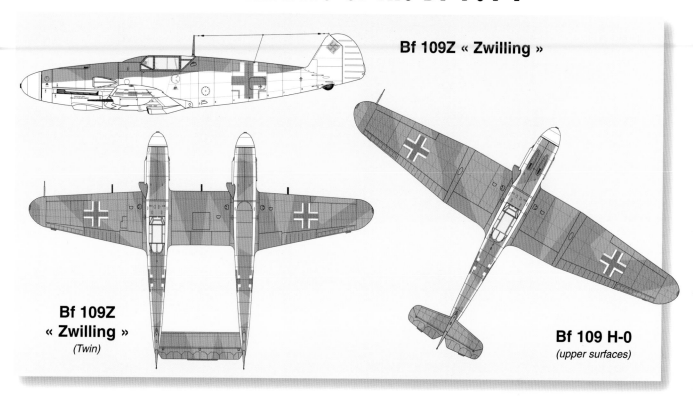

Bf 109Z « Zwilling »

Bf 109Z « Zwilling » (Twin)

Bf 109 H-0 (upper surfaces)

As mentioned above, the Bf 109F was often used as a flying test bed and also for some very varied research projects, particularly because it was more available after being replaced by the Gustav in the front line and because it resembled its successor.

It was fitted first with a BMW 801 radial, then a Jumo 213 with an annular radiator (a technical feature of the Fw 190), then with a V- type tail surfaces which resulted in bad lateral stability, especially when landing.

One of the most spectacular projects using the Friedrich was without doubt the Bf 109Z (for 'Zwilling'-Twin), a solution which had already been tried out on the Heinkel 111. It consisted of joining two 109F fuselages together by means of a new central wing section and a new tail section. The project was started at the end of 1942; the new aircraft retained the left-hand cockpit (the right-hand one was filled in and masked over), the four wing radiators but only the two outer undercarriage members.

The prototype was destroyed during an air raid when it was almost complete. The series production of what was to have been a heavy fighter (*Zerstörer*), armed with five 20 mm cannon, would have used *Gustav* fuselages since those of the 109F were no longer being produced at the time, but the project was finally abandoned at the beginning of 1944 without any new prototype being built.

The Friedrich was also widely used for the design studies of the Me 309. Different parts of the fighter were tried out on it: tricycle undercarriage, ventral radiator, pressurised cockpit, etc.

Finally, the only variant of these different attempts which was actually built was the Bf 109H, a high altitude fighter thought up at the beginning of 1943, using a Friedrich. A extra section of wing was installed at the wing root, the horizontal tail-plane was enlarged, whilst the armament and the engine were those of the F-4/Z equipped with power boost equipment. It was heavier than a standard Bf 109F and had a slightly higher top speed, and above all, could reach 14 000 metres (about 47 000 feet) thanks to its 39-foot wing span. A pre-production series of Bf 109H-0s was tried out operationally at Guyancourt aerodrome (France) but encountered a lot of wing flutter which caused several accidents.

A little later, a small number of production models (Bf 109H-1, based on the Gustav) were finally produced and used especially for armed reconnaissance missions over England in 1944, but in spite of their obvious qualities, they were abandoned in favour of the more promising Ta 152H.

ME 109G CAMOUFLAGE SCHEMES

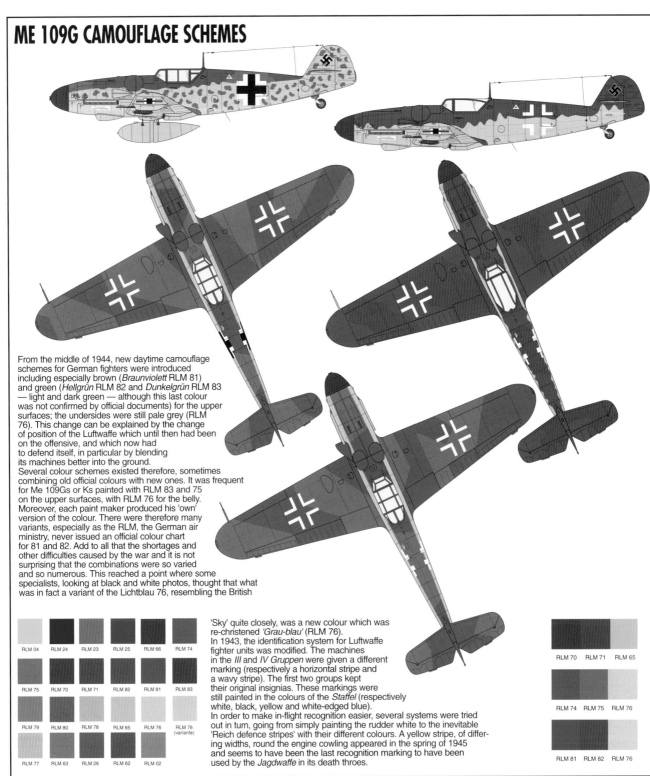

From the middle of 1944, new daytime camouflage schemes for German fighters were introduced including especially brown (*Braunviolett* RLM 81) and green (*Hellgrün* RLM 82 and *Dunkelgrün* RLM 83 — light and dark green — although this last colour was not confirmed by official documents) for the upper surfaces; the undersides were still pale grey (RLM 76). This change can be explained by the change of position of the Luftwaffe which until then had been on the offensive, and which now had to defend itself, in particular by blending its machines better into the ground.

Several colour schemes existed therefore, sometimes combining old official colours with new ones. It was frequent for Me 109Gs or Ks painted with RLM 83 and 75 on the upper surfaces, with RLM 76 for the belly. Moreover, each paint maker produced his 'own' version of the colour. There were therefore many variants, especially as the RLM, the German air ministry, never issued an official colour chart for 81 and 82. Add to all that the shortages and other difficulties caused by the war and it is not surprising that the combinations were so varied and so numerous. This reached a point where some specialists, looking at black and white photos, thought that what was in fact a variant of the Lichtblau 76, resembling the British

'Sky' quite closely, was a new colour which was re-christened *'Grau-blau'* (RLM 76).

In 1943, the identification system for Luftwaffe fighter units was modified. The machines in the *III* and *IV Gruppen* were given a different marking (respectively a horizontal stripe and a wavy stripe). The first two groups kept their original insignias. These markings were still painted in the colours of the *Staffel* (respectively white, black, yellow and white-edged blue).

In order to make in-flight recognition easier, several systems were tried out in turn, going from simply painting the rudder white to the inevitable 'Reich defence stripes' with their different colours. A yellow stripe, of differing widths, round the engine cowling appeared in the spring of 1945 and seems to have been the last recognition marking to have been used by the *Jagdwaffe* in its death throes.

RLM 04	RLM 24	RLM 23	RLM 25	RLM 66	RLM 74
RLM 75	RLM 70	RLM 71	RLM 82	RLM 81	RLM 83
RLM 79	RLM 80	RLM 78	RLM 65	RLM 76	RLM 76 (variante)
RLM 77	RLM 63	RLM 26	RLM 62	RLM 02	

RLM 70	RLM 71	RLM 65
RLM 74	RLM 75	RLM 76
RLM 81	RLM 82	RLM 76

Me 109 G for *GUSTAV*

With the *'Friedrich'*, the Bf 109 seemed to have reached its optimum limit, the basic concept having been taken as far as it would go. However, during the summer of 1941, since no immediate successor was available — the Me 209 which had been envisaged was finally not produced — the Messerschmitt engineers were given the order to modernise it and make it evolve.

Thus was the Bf 109G or *'Gustav'* created, built around the new Daimler-Benz DB 605. This was more powerful than its predecessors; and it was also heavier which meant reinforcing the airframe; this of course increased the total mass of the aircraft. There was just no time to re-think the plane and improve its aerodynamics or its structure. Only speed was considered, to the detriment of manoeuvrability and lightness, a choice which caused a lot of pilots to complain that this new version was not a step in the right direction.

Since the new engine was not available when the first variant, the G-0, was ready to be evaluated, the aircraft flew with an F-4 engine in the modified airframe of the new variant.

The differences between an end-of-series Friedrich and a beginning-of-series Gustav were scarcely noticeable, the absence of the little glass window sections on the side of the windshield being the only distinguishing feature.

The Bf 109G was not particularly better than its predecessors but it was the version which was produced most. More than 10 000 models in a whole host of different versions and variants came off the assembly lines practically until the end of the conflict.

On a more or less large scale, all German fighter units used the Gustav and the aeroplane equipped eight other countries' air forces, allied or not to Germany.

What was surprising about the Bf 109G was the incredibly large number of modifications it underwent during its long career, the final 1945-versions hardly resembling the machines which had been produced three years earlier. Apart from the changes made necessary by the use of a new engine, the way the war was going played an important part in the decision as to how the original con-

The G-6 was the most produced of all the Bf 109Gs and it was continually modified and improved. This machine was captured intact by the British and had been used for the defence of the Reich as evidenced by the fuselage stripe; it was equipped with one of the older hoods with supports, and was fitted with a larger tailfin made of wood.
(IWM)

cept should change. Messerschmitt's fighter had definitely become faster but it was faced with increasingly more solid, more effective and better-defended adversaries, namely the boxes of Allied B-17 and B-24 bombers.

Used in conjunction with the Luftwaffe's other *'star'*, the Fw 190 which was better-armed and more manoeuvrable, the Me 109G specialised in high-altitude combat, against the formations of huge Allied four-engined bombers. To increase its performance, various solutions were tried out and installed: more efficient engines of the AS type with power-boost or methanol-water injection giving increased speed for a short time; increasing range by using drop-tanks; increased firepower (by increasing the nose canon from 20 to 30 mm and the machine guns from 13 to 17 mm, using rocket-launchers or cannon installed in underwing trays), etc.

Modifications were carried out to improve the aircraft with its canopy (simplified mountings), its undercarriage (wider diameter wheels, lengthened tailwheel) or its tail (increased rudder surface). Twice the German authorities tried to put some order into this diversity of variants and models, first with the G-14 which was intended to incorporate all the different modifications which had been made to the G-6, then with the G-10 which was to have ensured the transition with the last variant, the 109K.

This plan failed because each one of these versions itself generated a whole series of variants which made the whole into an almost inextricable maze.

33

DIFFERENT TYPES OF BF 109G

G-0

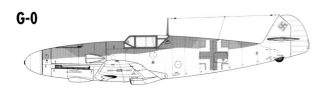

A dozen produced. Used the F-4. DB601E powerplant. Production series engine cowling, but without the extra intakes on the fuselage behind the propeller.

G-1

167 produced between May and July 1942.
Closely resembled the F-4. DB605A engine. Wide turbo-charger air intake, as on the last F-4s. Larger Fo 870 oil radiator.
Two little intakes placed on the fuselage just behind the propeller.
3-metre diameter VDM propeller, with wider blades rounded at the tips. Pressurised cockpit with a new armoured installation fitted into the moving part of the canopy. Side windshield glass panels removed. Canopy with reinforced and welded (formerly bolted) mountings.
Double-glazed windows filled with silicate gel granules to prevent humidity.
Tank opening placed on the left, between frames 2 and 3.
Wheel wells with rounded edges and extra doors (but these were never fitted)
Armament was identical to the F-4.
FuG VIIa and FuG 25 radio equipment with antenna fitted beneath the fuselage on frame 3.
There was no official tropicalised version, but some may have been modified in the field.
— *G-1/R2:* the 80 last machines produced by Messerschmitt. Lightened machines with a drop tank pylon and fitted with the GM-1 power boost system.

G-2

More than 1 500 produced (1587?) from May 1942 to February 1943. Identical to the G-1 but without the pressurising system. Pilot's seat entirely armoured. Cockpit ventilation intakes fitted instead of the windshield side glass panels (though this could vary)

G-2 Trop

— *G-2/Trop:* sand filter in front of the turbo-charger intake as on the F. On the left on a level with the cockpit, two support points for fitting a sunshade to protect the cockpit interior.
— *G-2/R1:* two underwing 300-litre drop tanks and an ETC pylon with jettisonable tailwheel under the fuselage. System was tried out successfully but never used. No production series

G-2/R-2

— *G-2/R2* reconnaissance variant with GM-1 power boost system and different camera models. Sometimes the canon was removed.

G-4

A non-pressurised version of the G-3. More than 1 240 machines produced between December 1942 and September 1943. A development of the G-2 with minor differences: radio apparatus and the position of the radio antenna. Bigger wheels (at first spoked then filled-in) and tailwheel to support the increased weight. Upper wing surface tear drop bumps. Retracting mechanism for the tailwheel removed.

G-4/R-2

— *G-4/R2* reconnaissance version. Cameras. Canon removed.
— *G-4/R4* reconnaissance version. Cameras. Engine-mounted machine guns removed and the openings sometimes filled in.
— *G-4/Trop* tropicalised version identical to the G-2/Trop.
— *G-4/U3* equipped with MW 50 methanol-water injection system giving increased power over short periods of time.

G-3

50 machines produced in January-February 1943. Pressurised variant (system identical to the G-1) otherwise like the G-4.
— *G-3/U2 high altitude fighter version with GM-1 power boost system and shorter propeller. No proof of it ever having been made.*

G-6

Produced in greatest numbers (12 000 machines) DB605A engine. Engine-mounted armament replaced by two MG 131 13-mm machine guns, with fairings to cover the breeches. Openings for the machine guns cut out not added. Small oval hatch on the fuselage between frames 8 and 9. In the summer 1943 'Galland Panzer' (bullet-proof glass replacing the armour plate to protect the pilot - the 'Galland Hood') installed at the end of 1943, the appearance of the 'Erla' canopy with simplified structural supports. Beginning of 1944: new tailfin with larger rudder. Lengthened tailwheel on the last models of the series. Circular radio antenna on the fuselage back.

G-6/R-2

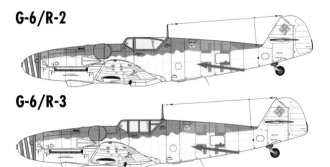

G-6/R-3

— *G-6/R2 reconnaissance version with Rb 50/30 cameras fitted in the fuselage (between frames 2 and 3).*
— *G-6/R3 ditto but with Rb 75/30 camera.*

G-6 Trop

— *G-6/Trop tropicalised version with sand filter and sunshade fittings on the left side, under the cockpit*
— *G-6/U2 fitted with the GM-1 power boost system.*
— *G-6/U3 with MW 50 methanol-water injection system.*

Specifications- G-6

Type
Single-seat fighter

Motorisation
One Daimler-Benz DB 605A-1 liquid-cooled 12-cylinder in-line engine.

Dimensions
Wingspan: *9.92 m*
Length: *9.02 m*
Height: *3.40 m*
Wing area: *16.05m²*

Weight (empty): *2 700kg*
Weight (loaded): *3 150kg*

Performances
Max. Speed: *623kph at 7 000m; 544kph at sea-level.*
Rate of Climb to 6 000m: *6 mins.*
Ceiling: *11 750 m*
Max. Ceiling: *12 100 m*

Armament
Two MG 131/13 13 mm machine guns with 300rpg. One MG 151/20 20 mm canon with 150 rounds.

G-6 (R3)

G-6/U-4

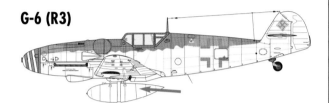

G-6 (Erla hood)

G-6 (bigger tailfin)

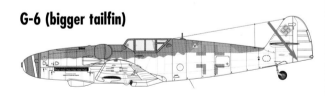

— *G-6/U4 with 30-mm MK 108 canon.*
— *G-6/U4N (sometimes simply called G-6/N) night fighter equipped with the Naxos FuG 350 radar detection (of allied bombers) system.*
— *G-6/U5 with MG 151/20 canon.*
— *G-6Y equipped with FuG 16ZY with ('Morane') whip antenna under the belly between the radiators.*
— *G-6AS with a DB605AS engine with a bigger turbo-charger for high-altitude use.*
Engine cradle modified and reinforced.
Front of fuselage redesigned. Bigger propeller.
Larger air intake for the turbo-charger.
Nearly always fitted with the Erla hood and the bigger tailfin. 200 actually produced but at least 600 conversions.

About 475 machines built at the same time as the G-6 from May 1943 to August 1944. Overall identical to the G-6 but with a pressurised cockpit. Position of MG 131 machine guns pushed the compressor to the right protected by a little bump under the machine gun fairings which had air intakes.
— **G-5/AS** with DB605AS powerplant.
— **G-5/R2** (or **G-5/U2**) reconnaissance variant with GM-1 power boost system.
— **G-5/R4** ditto but without the engine-mounted machine guns.
— **G-5Y** fitted with FuG 16zy radio.

Tactical reconnaissance version. Produced between August 1943 to the beginning of 1945. Overall identical to the G-6 but frames 5 and 6 reinforced to take miscellaneous photographic equipment with openings under the fuselage. Standard tailfin save rare exceptions. FuG 17 radio and radio antenna mast moved back to frames 3 and 4. Some machines without canon.
— **G-8/U2** fitted with GM-1 power boost system.
— **G-8/U3** fitted with MW 50 methanol-water injection system.
— **G-8/R2** fitted with Rb 50/30 camera.
— **G-8/R3** fitted with two Rb 32/7x9 cameras.
— **G-8/R5** fitted with two Rb 12.5/7x9 cameras.

G-12 transforming G-6

G-12 transforming G-2

G-12

Two-seater trainer made by transforming existing machines (G-2, 3, 4 and 6). Second seat placed behind the original one with movable hood and concave glass side sections. Reduced fuel load. Armament normally removed, though some machines did keep one or two machine guns.

G-14

G-14

More than 5 000 machines produced, not continuously (July 1944 to February 1945). Identical to the end-of-production G-6: DB605A engine, Erla hood, small or big tailfin, lengthened tailwheel, upper wing surface fairings square if wheels bigger. Only the radio antenna for the FuG 16Y - when this was installed - was moved to the left wing.
— **G-14/R2** reconnaissance variant, identical to the G-10/R2.
— **G-14/R6** a planned variant which was never made fitted with all-weather pilot instrumentation.

— **G-14/U4** fitted with MK 108 canon.

G-14 AS

— **G-14/AS** fitted with DB605AS engine some with larger Fo 987 oil radiator, otherwise identical to the G-6/AS.

G-10

G-10

About 2 600 built (October 1944- end of the war). No uniform version but a plethora of variants and combinations, as with the G-6 and the G-14: long or short tailwheel, wing fairings depending on the size of the wheels, big or small tail, radio masts, etc. Erla hood apparently was standard.
Machines were fitted with the DB605DM (with MW 50 system): a small bump on either side of the fuselage, under the first exhaust pipe and a larger oil radiator. Oil fillers placed higher up.
— **G-10/R2** fitted with Rb 50/30 camera in the fuselage and MW 50 system.
— **G-10/R5** fitted with Rb 12.5/7x9 camera.
— **G-10/R6** fitted with semi-automatic pilot for bad weather.
— **G-10/R7** fitted with underwing WGr.21 rocket-launchers.
— **G-10/U4** fitted with 30-mm canon and MW 50 system.

Five Rüstsätze existed for the Gustav although the different versions did not use them all. (N.B. a Rüstsatz - additional equipment - did not change the aircraft designation).
— **R1:** Bomb-launcher pylon ETC 500 IXb
— **R2:** Bomb-launcher pylon ETC 50/VIId
— **R3:** belly pylon and 300-litre drop tank.
— **R5:** two underwing gondolas containing an MK 108 30-mm canon.
— **R6:** two underwing gondolas containing an MG 151/20 20-mm canon.
— **R7:** Gonio navigational aid system (Peilrufanlage) with a circular antenna on the fuselage back

G-10 (R3)

FROM the G-1 to the G-4

It was in October 1941 that the first pre-production Gustavs, designated G-0, came off the assembly line. The engine which was to have equipped them, the DB 604A, was not yet available at that time and it was decided to fly them with the Bf 109F-4's DB601E installed in the new airframe which had been modified around the engine cowling to accommodate a larger oil radiator fairing.

Several incidents, some of them serious, initially marred the short operational career of the production series; two cooling fairings for the plugs and the gun breeches were added

This G-4 from the I./JG 27 'Afrika' was photographed at Leeuwarden (Holland) in the spring of 1943. The insignia can be clearly seen on the fuselage. In order to increase its firepower, two 20 mm canon were installed in underwing gondolas.
(BA)

first Gustavs sent to the east enabled the Germans to maintain air superiority which they had won a year earlier with the Friedrich.

Taking part in the battle of Stalingrad - the last fighter to leave the besieged town was a G-2 of the JG 3 on 2 February 1942, a few days before the surrender, the Gustav was confronted with a worsening situation at the beginning of this new year because of the appearance of the Yakovlev 7s and 9s. However the *'Experten'* (aces) still managed to improve their scores with the Me 109, especially a certain Emil Hartmann, who won the first of his

to each side of the engine cowling, just behind the propeller. Their purpose was to prevent the radiator oil which was vaporised by the very hot engine from catching fire, as had already been the case. This improvement was maintained for all the Gustavs which followed but this version was to suffer from oil pressure problems throughout its career.

The G-1 was produced from the spring of 1942 and arrived at the front in June of the same year. Overall this production series was similar to the F-4, especially the armament which was identical; but its pressurised cockpit meant the disappearance of the lateral windshield panes and the strengthening of the canopy structure. The new engine, the DB605A, was a variant of the DB601E with a higher compression rate and a larger bore, and its engine turnover was higher.

A few more than 160 G-1s were built and were attributed as a priority to units facing the heavy Allied bomber formations over the Channel or North Africa. In the summer of 1942, the first squadron specialised in high altitude interception, the 11./JG 2 equipped with G-1/R2s, 'lightened' by getting rid of some of the armour, carrying a 300-litre drop tank and equipped with GM-1 power boost. A few weeks later, another high altitude Staffel was formed, the 11./JG 26, operating over the Channel at first before being transferred to the Mediterranean front.

Produced at the same time as the G-1, the G-2 was in fact built in greater numbers and delivered to the units before it, from June 1942. This was in fact a non-pressurised version of the G-1, being distinguishable by the cockpit ventilation intakes below the windshield, located differently depending on the machine. It was headquarters and the first group of the JG-2 which used this type first, from the end of spring 1942. Walther Oesau, the unit's famous *Kommodore* preferred however using his Fw 190. The G-2 spread gradually within the Jagdwaffe and was used by all the units. The

352 victories in November 1942.

Northern Africa was another theatre where the first Gustavs distinguished themselves; a tropicalised version of the G-2 was made with an extra sand filter but also two anchor points which were for fitting… a sunshade, a very useful accessory for reducing the interior temperature of the cockpit of a fighter on stand-by out in the sun. The first G-2/Trop. arrived in North Africa at the end of June 1942 but many were lost in the retreat following the battle of El Alamein. Finland was among the foreign buyers of the 109G-2, purchasing sixteen at the beginning of 1943 in order to face the threat from the new Russian La-5s. One of the most original variants was without doubt the G-2/R1, a fighter-bomber fitted with two underwing 300 litre drop tanks and an ETC 500 pylon under the fuselage and extra jettisonable landing gear. This enabled the aircraft to have the ground clearance necessary for the extra system underneath the fuselage. The system was tried out successfully but was never developed.

Developed from the G-2 and conceived particularly as a fighter, the G-4 version came out next on a large scale production reaching some 1 200 machines. It was very similar to the G-2 and it was only the radio equipment with its vertical antenna wire placed further back which distinguished them. During the production run, larger wheels were fitted which meant fitting water-drop shaped fairings on the upper wing surfaces which gave the aircraft its nickname *'Beule'* - Hump - which it kept until the end of the war. The tailwheel was lengthened which meant that the retracting mechanism was removed. Many G-4s were used for reconnaissance, a specific variant, the G-4/R3 being specially produced for long distance reconnaissance. In January 1943, while the G-4 production started, Messerschmitt made a short series of fifty G-3s which were sent to the high altitude fighter units (11./JG2, 11./JG 26 and 11./JG 54) fighting in the west. These variants were in fact pressurised versions, like the G-1, but with the modifications of the G-4.

Me 109G-1 and G-2 IN THE LUFTWAFFE

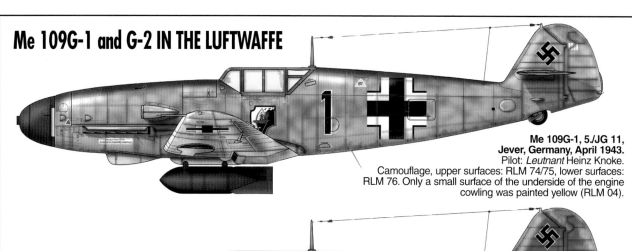

**Me 109G-1, 5./JG 11,
Jever, Germany, April 1943.**
Pilot: *Leutnant* Heinz Knoke.
Camouflage, upper surfaces: RLM 74/75, lower surfaces:
RLM 76. Only a small surface of the underside of the engine
cowling was painted yellow (RLM 04).

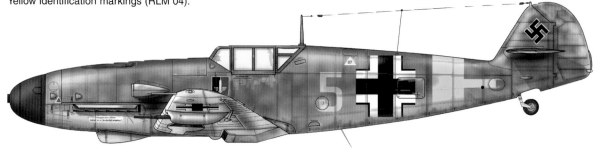

Me 109G-2, 8./JG 52, Caucasus (Soviet Union), September 1942.
Pilot: *Oberleutnant* Günther Rall.
Camouflage, upper surfaces: RLM 74/75, lower surfaces: RLM 76.
Yellow identification markings (RLM 04).

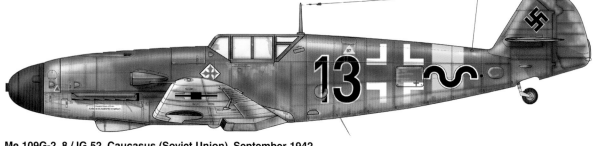

Me 109G-2, 6./JG 52, Russian Front, October 1942
Pilot: *Leutnant* Walter *'Graf Punski'* Krupinski.
Camouflage, upper surfaces: RLM 74/75,
with extra RLM 71 blotches and lower surfaces: RLM 76.
Yellow identification markings (RLM 04).

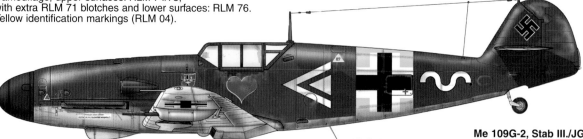

**Me 109G-2, Stab III./JG 52,
'Grünherz', Lissino, Soviet Union, September 1942.**
Pilot: *Hauptmann* Reinhard Seiler
Camouflage, upper surfaces: RLM 70/71, lower surfaces: RLM 76. Yellow identification markings (RLM 04).
This aircraft was armed with two MG 151/20 20-mm cannon in underwing gondolas (*Rüstsatz* R6).

THE Me 109 G-2 IN THE LUFTWAFFE

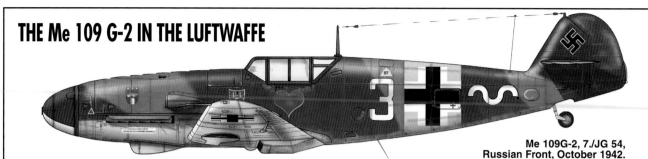

Me 109G-2, 7./JG 54,
Russian Front, October 1942.
Pilot: *Oberfeldwebel* Karl-Heinz Kempf.
Camouflage, upper surfaces with wide RLM 70, 71 and 02 stripes, lower surfaces: RLM 76.
Yellow identification markings (RLM 04).

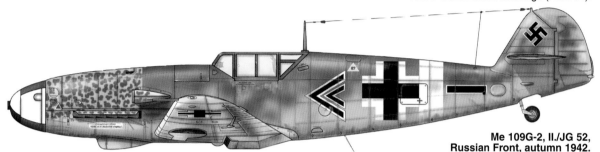

Me 109G-2, II./JG 52,
Russian Front, autumn 1942.
Pilot: *Hauptmann* Johannes Steinhoff, *Gruppenkommandeur.*
Camouflage, upper surfaces: RLM 74/75, lower surfaces: RLM 76. Yellow identification markings (RLM 04).
The upper surface of the engine cowling is camouflaged differently and this was to be found on other machines in the flight at the time.

Me 109G-2, 6./JG 5 '*Eismeer*',
Petsamo, Finland, March 1943.
Pilot: *Oberleutnant* Heinrich Ehrler.
This unit operated in the northern part of the Russian Front and was camouflaged differently in order to blend better into the vast wooded and snow-covered expanses. This camouflage was made up of green blotches on a whiter background with RLM 76 lower surfaces.

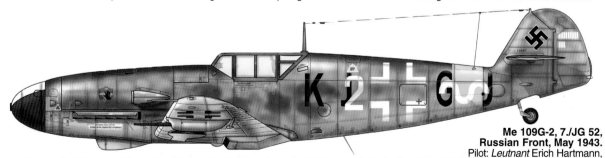

Me 109G-2, 7./JG 52,
Russian Front, May 1943.
Pilot: *Leutnant* Erich Hartmann,
the greatest German '*Expert*' (and the greatest fighter-pilot in the history of aviation) with a tally of 352 kills, aged only 21 at the time...
Camouflage, upper surfaces: RLM 74/75, lower surfaces: RLM 76. Yellow identification markings (RLM 04).
The factory code number is still visible under the tactical identification markings.

THE Me 109 G-2 IN THE LUFTWAFFE

Me 109G-2, JG 5, Norway, winter 1943.
In order to hide it better, the machine's original upper
dark green RLM 71 camouflage has been partly covered with irregular RLM 76 light grey,
or white, coil-like stripes. Lower surfaces: RLM 76.

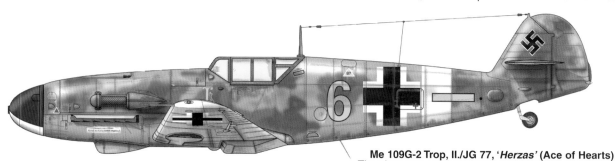

Me 109G-2 Trop, II./JG 77, 'Herzas' (Ace of Hearts)
The plane was completely painted in light blue RLM 78,
the upper surfaces were unevenly daubed with green and sand (RLM 80 and 79).

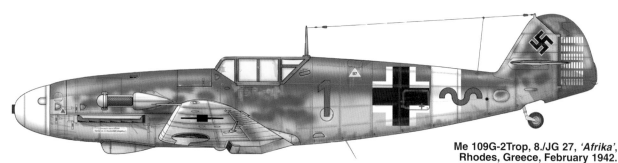

**Me 109G-2Trop, 8./JG 27, 'Afrika',
Rhodes, Greece, February 1942.**
Pilot: *Hauptmann* Werner Schroer, *Staffelkapitän*.
Camouflage, upper surfaces: RLM 74/75, lower surfaces: RLM 76. The tail was painted red (RLM 23 or red anticorrosion primer).

**Me 109G-2 Trop, 2./JG 77,
Gabès, Tunisia, 1943.**
The normal camouflage, RLM 79 above and RLM 78 below,
has been made up with green (or Italian dark green) wavy RLM 80 lines.
White identification markings (RLM 21). The position of the unit insignia, at the rear of the fuselage was unusual.

THE Me 109G-2 IN FOREIGN COLOURS

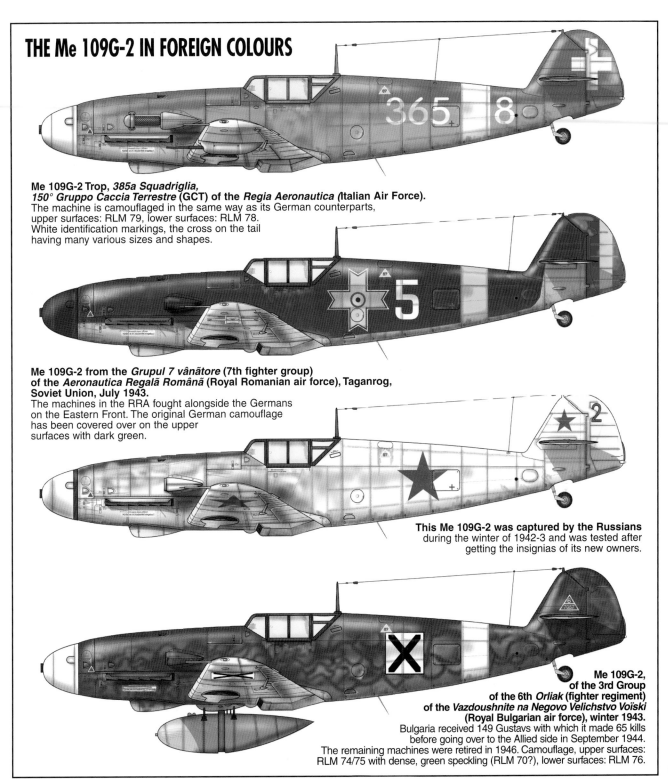

Me 109G-2 Trop, *385a Squadriglia,*
150° Gruppo Caccia Terrestre **(GCT) of the** *Regia Aeronautica* **(Italian Air Force).**
The machine is camouflaged in the same way as its German counterparts,
upper surfaces: RLM 79, lower surfaces: RLM 78.
White identification markings, the cross on the tail
having many various sizes and shapes.

Me 109G-2 from the *Grupul 7 vânãtore* **(7th fighter group)**
of the *Aeronautica Regalã Românã* **(Royal Romanian air force), Taganrog,**
Soviet Union, July 1943.
The machines in the RRA fought alongside the Germans
on the Eastern Front. The original German camouflage
has been covered over on the upper
surfaces with dark green.

This Me 109G-2 was captured by the Russians
during the winter of 1942-3 and was tested after
getting the insignias of its new owners.

Me 109G-2,
of the 3rd Group
of the 6th *Orliak* **(fighter regiment)**
of the *Vazdoushnite na Negovo Velichstvo Voïski*
(Royal Bulgarian air force), winter 1943.
Bulgaria received 149 Gustavs with which it made 65 kills
before going over to the Allied side in September 1944.
The remaining machines were retired in 1946. Camouflage, upper surfaces:
RLM 74/75 with dense, green speckling (RLM 70?), lower surfaces: RLM 76.

G-5 and G-6

The G-6 appeared chronologically before the G-5 and was produced in greater numbers. It is estimated that 12 000 machines of all variant types came off the production lines, over a very long time, from the beginning of 1943 to the end of 1944.

This new *Gustav* model was conceived originally in answer to the triple problem posed by the preceding versions: how to reconcile weak armament (a problem already encountered with the 'F'), a higher speed which meant less time in front of the target (about one second) with opponents like the Allied four-engined bombers which were increasingly more solid? To answer this question, it was decided to increase the fixed armament, copying the Fw 190 with its two machine guns and its cannon.

The two engine-mounted 7.92 mm MG 17 machine guns were replaced by 13 mm MG 131 machine guns. The breech feeders of these new heavy weapons could not be housed under the standard engine cowling and it was necessary to protect them by means of two almost-circular bumps, placed on the cowling, which gave the new Gustav an easily recognisable new look. But this armament increase also meant a weight increase, which reduced its performance even more — hardly what the machine needed.

To make up for this, the GM-1 power boost system, used occasionally on preceding models, was fitted as standard on most machines.

Another feature of the G-6 was the presence of a little oval trap door on the left hand side of the fuselage between frames 8 and 9 and which was maintained on all subsequent Gustavs. The basic idea behind the Gustav was to produce a fighter which could be modified and take different engines depending on the type of mission it was going to be given. This version was produced in scores of different variants, from the ones with a windshield with simplified mountings, called 'Erla', to those with reinforced armour for the pilot's seat, and including those with different antenna masts and wire, a lengthened non-retractable tailwheel, etc. On this version a larger tail fin was fitted for the first time. Instead of the inverted 'L' shape of all previous 109 models, this version had a straight rudder.

In order to improve the plane's performance at high altitude where it excelled naturally, a new version, designated G-6/AS, started to come off the production lines at the beginning of 1944. The original DB605A was fitted with the same turbo-compressor as that of the DB603 and became the DB605AS. In order to fit the new engine into the fuselage, some modifications had to be made to the airframe which in turn meant redesigning the engine cowling. So the two bumps on the sides disappeared, replaced

by longer semi-circular asymmetric profiled fairings on both sides housing the engine cradle and the gun feeds.

Concurrently with G-6 production, a pressurised version, designated G-5, was also brought out but on a smaller scale (about 475 machines) from May 1943 to August 1944. In comparison with the basic model, the only important modification was the position of the air compressor, now on the right instead of on the left to make room for the new machine guns (with a little bump on the cowling to cover them).

The first G-6s were sent to the Mediterranean sector in February 1943 to serve in JG 53 and 77, and II./JG 27 and II./JG 51. A short while later the Reich defence units and those operating in Western Europe were supplied with this new machine. Then the squadrons on the Eastern front were equipped with the G-6, deliveries occurring at the same rate as that of production. From August 1943, some G-6s were armed with two underwing WGr 21 21 cm rocket tubes in order to be more effective against the Allied bomber formations. These *'Pulk Zerstörer'* (formation destroyers) were used particularly on 14 October 1943 against the raid on Schweinfurt, where they inflicted heavy losses on the Allies. During the following months, the G-6 was used increasingly to defend German territory, in high altitude attacks on the Allied fighters escorting the bomber box formations, leaving the Fw 190s which were far more effective at lower altitudes to attack the bomber boxes. Even though the German Army had left North African soil by the time that the G-6 reached the fighter units, quite a number of machines were tropicalised by adding an extra sand filter which turned out to be particularly effective in the dust of southern Russia, Sicily and southern Italy. One of the most original uses that the G-6 was put to was that of the *'Wilde Sau'* (Wild Boar), a group of specialised units in the *30. Jagddivision* (JG 300, 301 and 302) whose job was to attack the bombers which stood out against the light of the searchlights and the fires during night raids. The *30. Jagddivision* was disbanded in March 1944 after having suffered far too many losses mainly because of the lack of radio help, particularly in heavy weather, when the German pilots preferred to bale out rather than risk the danger of landing at night.

Four Bf 109G-6s from JG 104, a training unit bearing individual coloured numbers on the fuselage instead of the normal markings kept for combat units. The aircraft in the foreground is fitted with the simplified 'Erla' hood. *(BA)*

THE Me 109G-6 IN THE LUFTWAFFE

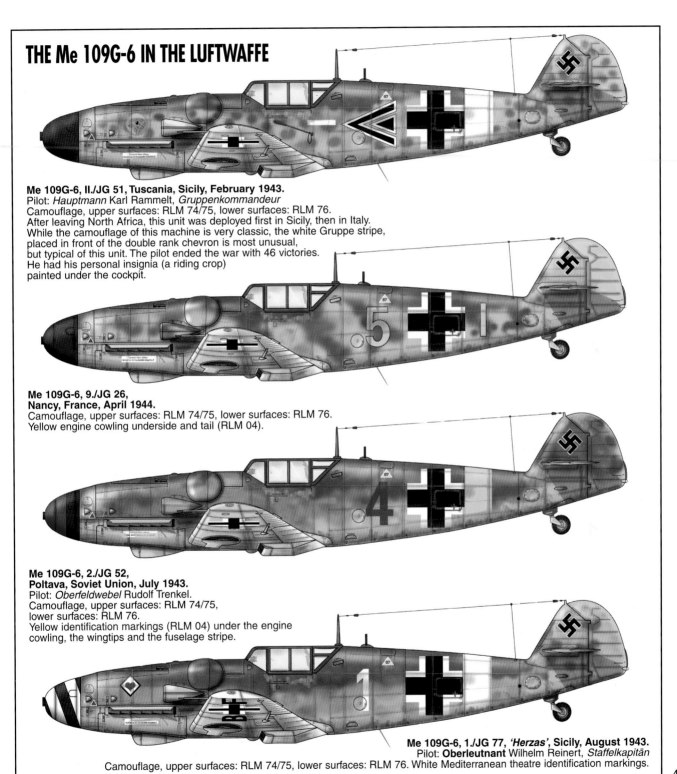

Me 109G-6, II./JG 51, Tuscania, Sicily, February 1943.
Pilot: *Hauptmann* Karl Rammelt, *Gruppenkommandeur*
Camouflage, upper surfaces: RLM 74/75, lower surfaces: RLM 76.
After leaving North Africa, this unit was deployed first in Sicily, then in Italy.
While the camouflage of this machine is very classic, the white Gruppe stripe,
placed in front of the double rank chevron is most unusual,
but typical of this unit. The pilot ended the war with 46 victories.
He had his personal insignia (a riding crop)
painted under the cockpit.

Me 109G-6, 9./JG 26,
Nancy, France, April 1944.
Camouflage, upper surfaces: RLM 74/75, lower surfaces: RLM 76.
Yellow engine cowling underside and tail (RLM 04).

Me 109G-6, 2./JG 52,
Poltava, Soviet Union, July 1943.
Pilot: *Oberfeldwebel* Rudolf Trenkel.
Camouflage, upper surfaces: RLM 74/75,
lower surfaces: RLM 76.
Yellow identification markings (RLM 04) under the engine
cowling, the wingtips and the fuselage stripe.

Me 109G-6, 1./JG 77, *'Herzas'*, Sicily, August 1943.
Pilot: **Oberleutnant** Wilhelm Reinert, *Staffelkapitän*
Camouflage, upper surfaces: RLM 74/75, lower surfaces: RLM 76. White Mediterranean theatre identification markings.

43

THE Me 109G-6 IN THE LUFTWAFFE

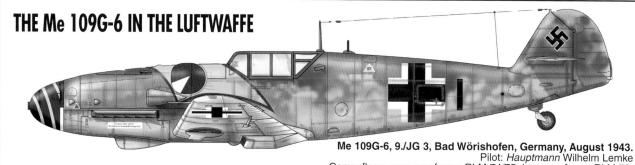

Me 109G-6, 9./JG 3, Bad Wörishofen, Germany, August 1943.
Pilot: *Hauptmann* Wilhelm Lemke
Camouflage, upper surfaces: RLM 74/75, lower surfaces: RLM 76.

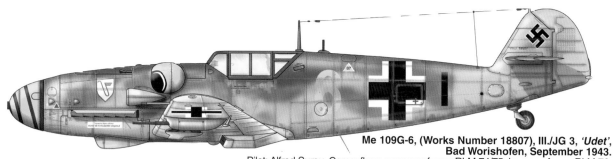

**Me 109G-6, (Works Number 18807), III./JG 3, *'Udet'*,
Bad Worishofen, September 1943.**
Pilot: Alfred Surau. Camouflage, upper surfaces: RLM 74/75, lower surfaces: RLM 76.
Most of the machines in this unit bore original decorations on all the fuselage bumps, here a rather stylised eye.
According to some sources, the tally of kills, in this case painted orange could also have been red.

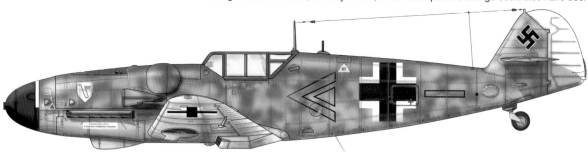

Me 109G-6, Stab of II./JG 3, Schipol (Holland), November 1943.
Pilot: *Major* Kurt Brändle.
Camouflage, upper surfaces: RLM 74/75, lower surfaces: RLM 76.
The lower part of the engine cowling was painted yellow
and the rudder, white. JG 3 was nicknamed *'Udet'* in honour
of the famous German pilot and its insignia is a stylised 'U'.

**Me 109G-6,
'Works Number
26065', 7 ./JG3,
Bad Worishofen, Germany, October 1943.** Camouflage,
upper surfaces: RLM 74/75, lower surfaces: RLM 76.
As the planes in the group all had their own special decorations
over the engine-mounted gun breech fairings, this *Staffel* bore a comet which
spread itself out in front of the windshield. Used in defence of German territory,
this Gustav was equipped with WGr.21 rocket launchers under the wings.

THE Me 109G-6 IN THE LUFTWAFFE

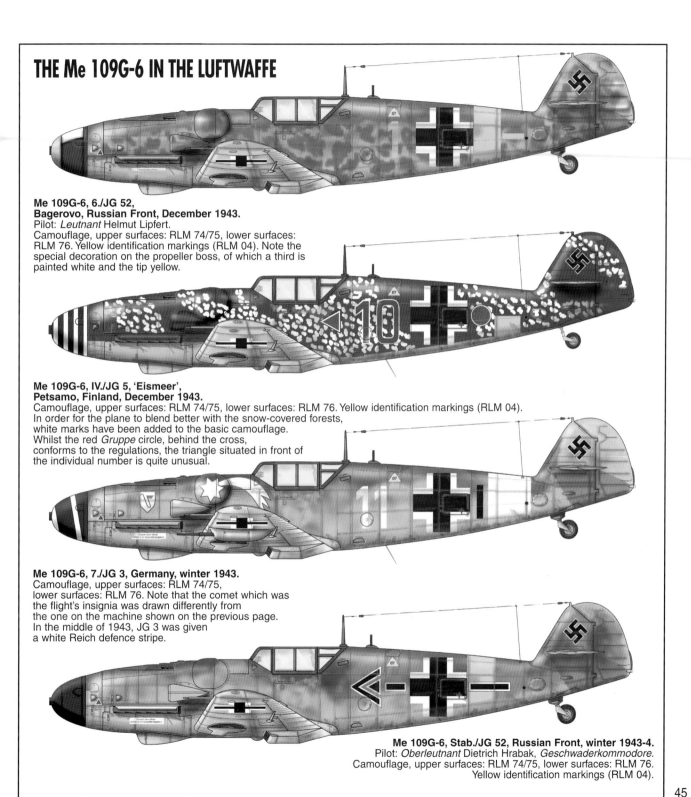

Me 109G-6, 6./JG 52,
Bagerovo, Russian Front, December 1943.
Pilot: *Leutnant* Helmut Lipfert.
Camouflage, upper surfaces: RLM 74/75, lower surfaces:
RLM 76. Yellow identification markings (RLM 04). Note the
special decoration on the propeller boss, of which a third is
painted white and the tip yellow.

Me 109G-6, IV./JG 5, 'Eismeer',
Petsamo, Finland, December 1943.
Camouflage, upper surfaces: RLM 74/75, lower surfaces: RLM 76. Yellow identification markings (RLM 04).
In order for the plane to blend better with the snow-covered forests,
white marks have been added to the basic camouflage.
Whilst the red *Gruppe* circle, behind the cross,
conforms to the regulations, the triangle situated in front of
the individual number is quite unusual.

Me 109G-6, 7./JG 3, Germany, winter 1943.
Camouflage, upper surfaces: RLM 74/75,
lower surfaces: RLM 76. Note that the comet which was
the flight's insignia was drawn differently from
the one on the machine shown on the previous page.
In the middle of 1943, JG 3 was given
a white Reich defence stripe.

Me 109G-6, Stab./JG 52, Russian Front, winter 1943-4.
Pilot: *Oberleutnant* Dietrich Hrabak, *Geschwaderkommodore*.
Camouflage, upper surfaces: RLM 74/75, lower surfaces: RLM 76.
Yellow identification markings (RLM 04).

45

THE Me 109G-6 IN THE LUFTWAFFE

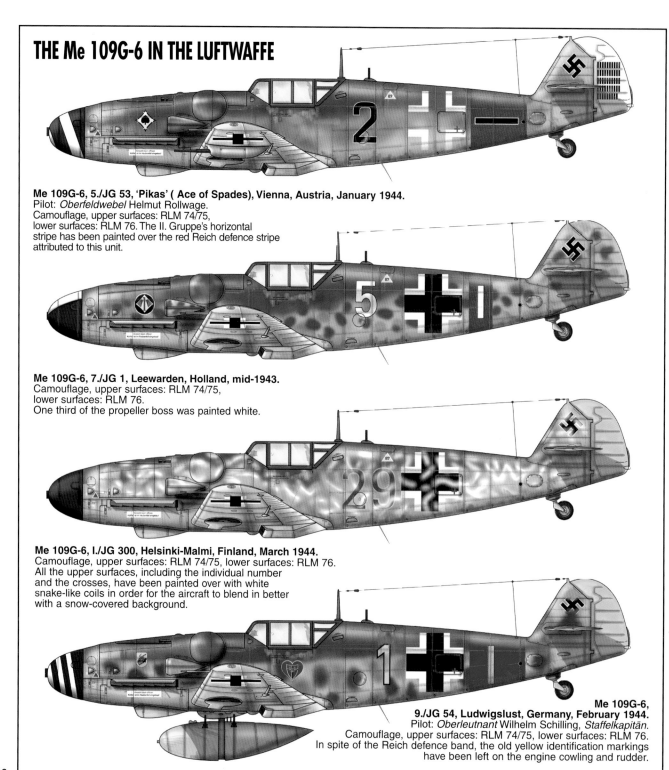

Me 109G-6, 5./JG 53, 'Pikas' (Ace of Spades), Vienna, Austria, January 1944.
Pilot: *Oberfeldwebel* Helmut Rollwage.
Camouflage, upper surfaces: RLM 74/75,
lower surfaces: RLM 76. The II. Gruppe's horizontal
stripe has been painted over the red Reich defence stripe
attributed to this unit.

Me 109G-6, 7./JG 1, Leewarden, Holland, mid-1943.
Camouflage, upper surfaces: RLM 74/75,
lower surfaces: RLM 76.
One third of the propeller boss was painted white.

Me 109G-6, I./JG 300, Helsinki-Malmi, Finland, March 1944.
Camouflage, upper surfaces: RLM 74/75, lower surfaces: RLM 76.
All the upper surfaces, including the individual number
and the crosses, have been painted over with white
snake-like coils in order for the aircraft to blend in better
with a snow-covered background.

**Me 109G-6,
9./JG 54, Ludwigslust, Germany, February 1944.**
Pilot: *Oberleutnant* Wilhelm Schilling, *Staffelkapitän*.
Camouflage, upper surfaces: RLM 74/75, lower surfaces: RLM 76.
In spite of the Reich defence band, the old yellow identification markings
have been left on the engine cowling and rudder.

THE Me 109G-6 IN THE LUFTWAFFE

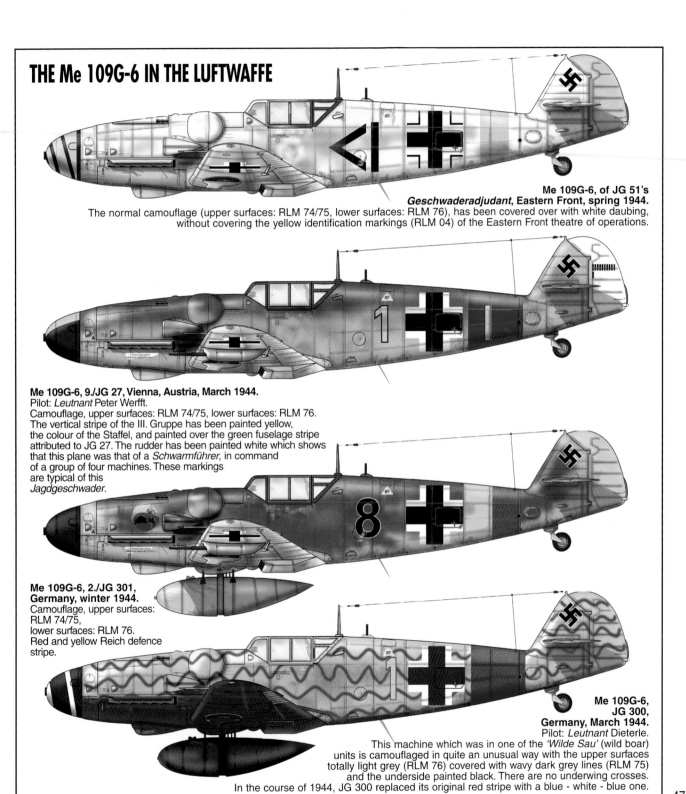

Me 109G-6, of JG 51's
***Geschwaderadjudant*, Eastern Front, spring 1944.**
The normal camouflage (upper surfaces: RLM 74/75, lower surfaces: RLM 76), has been covered over with white daubing, without covering the yellow identification markings (RLM 04) of the Eastern Front theatre of operations.

Me 109G-6, 9./JG 27, Vienna, Austria, March 1944.
Pilot: *Leutnant* Peter Werfft.
Camouflage, upper surfaces: RLM 74/75, lower surfaces: RLM 76.
The vertical stripe of the III. Gruppe has been painted yellow,
the colour of the Staffel, and painted over the green fuselage stripe
attributed to JG 27. The rudder has been painted white which shows
that this plane was that of a *Schwarmführer*, in command
of a group of four machines. These markings
are typical of this
Jagdgeschwader.

Me 109G-6, 2./JG 301,
Germany, winter 1944.
Camouflage, upper surfaces:
RLM 74/75,
lower surfaces: RLM 76.
Red and yellow Reich defence
stripe.

Me 109G-6,
JG 300,
Germany, March 1944.
Pilot: *Leutnant* Dieterle.
This machine which was in one of the *'Wilde Sau'* (wild boar)
units is camouflaged in quite an unusual way with the upper surfaces
totally light grey (RLM 76) covered with wavy dark grey lines (RLM 75)
and the underside painted black. There are no underwing crosses.
In the course of 1944, JG 300 replaced its original red stripe with a blue - white - blue one.

47

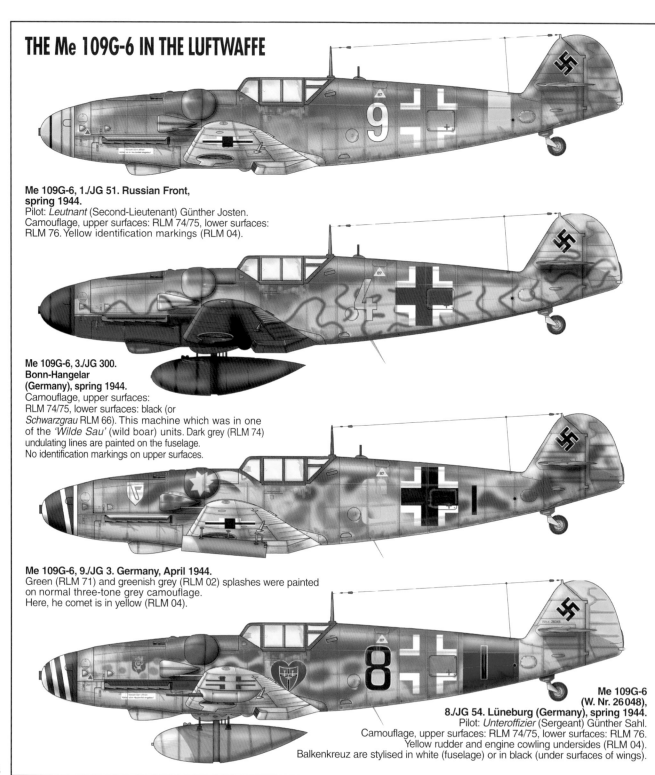

THE Me 109G-6 IN THE LUFTWAFFE

**Me 109G-6, 1./JG 51. Russian Front,
spring 1944.**
Pilot: *Leutnant* (Second-Lieutenant) Günther Josten.
Camouflage, upper surfaces: RLM 74/75, lower surfaces:
RLM 76. Yellow identification markings (RLM 04).

**Me 109G-6, 3./JG 300.
Bonn-Hangelar
(Germany), spring 1944.**
Camouflage, upper surfaces:
RLM 74/75, lower surfaces: black (or
Schwarzgrau RLM 66). This machine which was in one
of the *'Wilde Sau'* (wild boar) units. Dark grey (RLM 74)
undulating lines are painted on the fuselage.
No identification markings on upper surfaces.

Me 109G-6, 9./JG 3. Germany, April 1944.
Green (RLM 71) and greenish grey (RLM 02) splashes were painted
on normal three-tone grey camouflage.
Here, he comet is in yellow (RLM 04).

**Me 109G-6
(W. Nr. 26 048),
8./JG 54. Lüneburg (Germany), spring 1944.**
Pilot: *Unteroffizier* (Sergeant) Günther Sahl.
Camouflage, upper surfaces: RLM 74/75, lower surfaces: RLM 76.
Yellow rudder and engine cowling undersides (RLM 04).
Balkenkreuz are stylised in white (fuselage) or in black (under surfaces of wings).

THE Me 109G-6 IN THE LUFTWAFFE

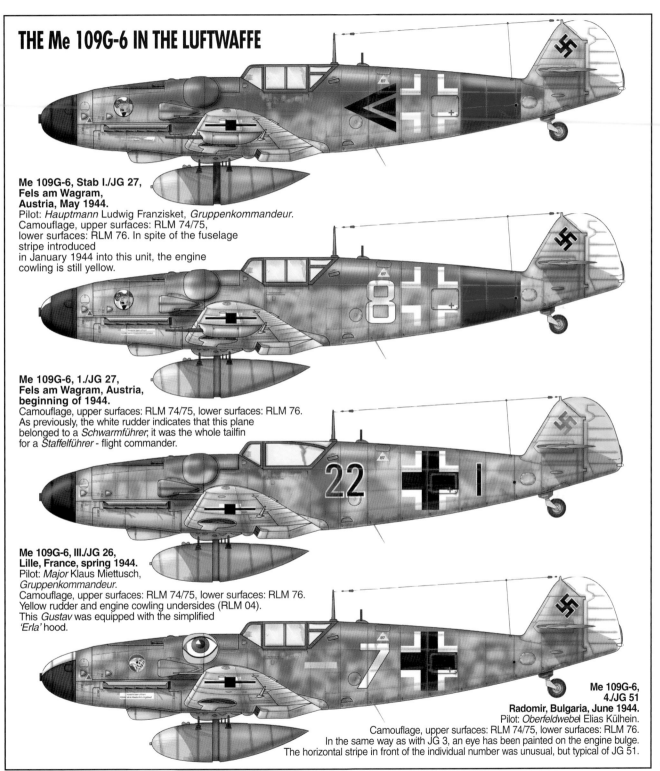

**Me 109G-6, Stab I./JG 27,
Fels am Wagram,
Austria, May 1944.**
Pilot: *Hauptmann* Ludwig Franzisket, *Gruppenkommandeur*.
Camouflage, upper surfaces: RLM 74/75,
lower surfaces: RLM 76. In spite of the fuselage
stripe introduced
in January 1944 into this unit, the engine
cowling is still yellow.

**Me 109G-6, 1./JG 27,
Fels am Wagram, Austria,
beginning of 1944.**
Camouflage, upper surfaces: RLM 74/75, lower surfaces: RLM 76.
As previously, the white rudder indicates that this plane
belonged to a *Schwarmführer*; it was the whole tailfin
for a *Staffelführer* - flight commander.

**Me 109G-6, III./JG 26,
Lille, France, spring 1944.**
Pilot: *Major* Klaus Miettusch,
Gruppenkommandeur.
Camouflage, upper surfaces: RLM 74/75, lower surfaces: RLM 76.
Yellow rudder and engine cowling undersides (RLM 04).
This *Gustav* was equipped with the simplified
'Erla' hood.

**Me 109G-6,
4./JG 51
Radomir, Bulgaria, June 1944.**
Pilot: *Oberfeldwebel* Elias Külhein.
Camouflage, upper surfaces: RLM 74/75, lower surfaces: RLM 76.
In the same way as with JG 3, an eye has been painted on the engine bulge.
The horizontal stripe in front of the individual number was unusual, but typical of JG 51.

THE Me 109G-6 IN THE LUFTWAFFE

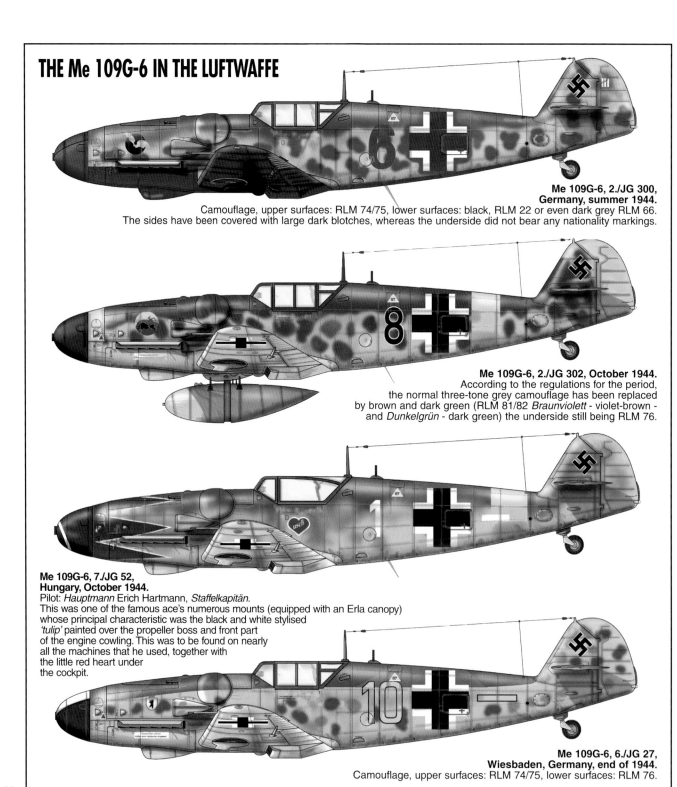

**Me 109G-6, 2./JG 300,
Germany, summer 1944.**
Camouflage, upper surfaces: RLM 74/75, lower surfaces: black, RLM 22 or even dark grey RLM 66.
The sides have been covered with large dark blotches, whereas the underside did not bear any nationality markings.

Me 109G-6, 2./JG 302, October 1944.
According to the regulations for the period,
the normal three-tone grey camouflage has been replaced
by brown and dark green (RLM 81/82 *Braunviolett* - violet-brown -
and *Dunkelgrün* - dark green) the underside still being RLM 76.

**Me 109G-6, 7./JG 52,
Hungary, October 1944.**
Pilot: *Hauptmann* Erich Hartmann, *Staffelkapitän*.
This was one of the famous ace's numerous mounts (equipped with an Erla canopy)
whose principal characteristic was the black and white stylised
'tulip' painted over the propeller boss and front part
of the engine cowling. This was to be found on nearly
all the machines that he used, together with
the little red heart under
the cockpit.

**Me 109G-6, 6./JG 27,
Wiesbaden, Germany, end of 1944.**
Camouflage, upper surfaces: RLM 74/75, lower surfaces: RLM 76.

THE Me 109G-6 TROPICALISED

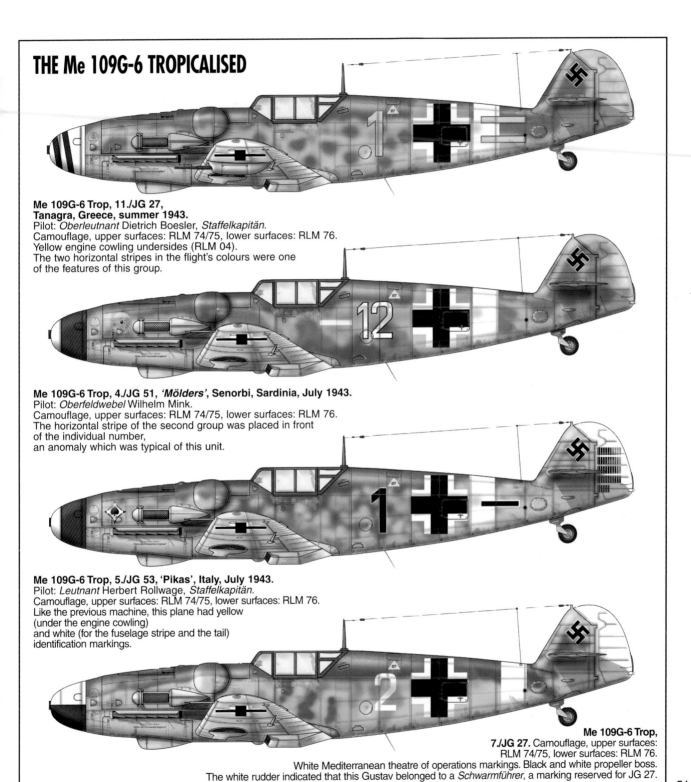

Me 109G-6 Trop, 11./JG 27,
Tanagra, Greece, summer 1943.
Pilot: *Oberleutnant* Dietrich Boesler, *Staffelkapitän*.
Camouflage, upper surfaces: RLM 74/75, lower surfaces: RLM 76.
Yellow engine cowling undersides (RLM 04).
The two horizontal stripes in the flight's colours were one
of the features of this group.

Me 109G-6 Trop, 4./JG 51, *'Mölders'*, Senorbi, Sardinia, July 1943.
Pilot: *Oberfeldwebel* Wilhelm Mink.
Camouflage, upper surfaces: RLM 74/75, lower surfaces: RLM 76.
The horizontal stripe of the second group was placed in front
of the individual number,
an anomaly which was typical of this unit.

Me 109G-6 Trop, 5./JG 53, 'Pikas', Italy, July 1943.
Pilot: *Leutnant* Herbert Rollwage, *Staffelkapitän*.
Camouflage, upper surfaces: RLM 74/75, lower surfaces: RLM 76.
Like the previous machine, this plane had yellow
(under the engine cowling)
and white (for the fuselage stripe and the tail)
identification markings.

Me 109G-6 Trop,
7./JG 27. Camouflage, upper surfaces:
RLM 74/75, lower surfaces: RLM 76.
White Mediterranean theatre of operations markings. Black and white propeller boss.
The white rudder indicated that this Gustav belonged to a *Schwarmführer*, a marking reserved for JG 27.

51

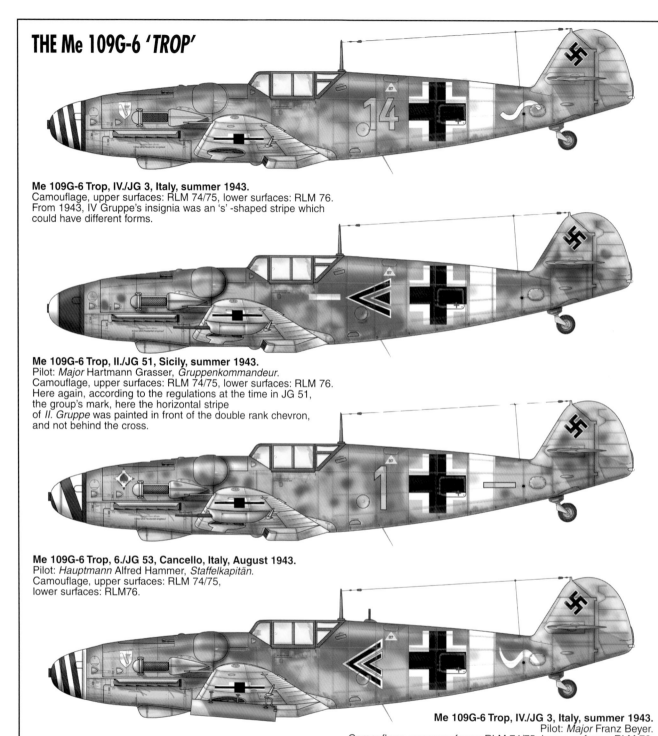

THE Me 109G-6 'TROP'

Me 109G-6 Trop, IV./JG 3, Italy, summer 1943.
Camouflage, upper surfaces: RLM 74/75, lower surfaces: RLM 76.
From 1943, IV Gruppe's insignia was an 's' -shaped stripe which
could have different forms.

Me 109G-6 Trop, II./JG 51, Sicily, summer 1943.
Pilot: *Major* Hartmann Grasser, *Gruppenkommandeur.*
Camouflage, upper surfaces: RLM 74/75, lower surfaces: RLM 76.
Here again, according to the regulations at the time in JG 51,
the group's mark, here the horizontal stripe
of *II. Gruppe* was painted in front of the double rank chevron,
and not behind the cross.

Me 109G-6 Trop, 6./JG 53, Cancello, Italy, August 1943.
Pilot: *Hauptmann* Alfred Hammer, *Staffelkapitän.*
Camouflage, upper surfaces: RLM 74/75,
lower surfaces: RLM76.

Me 109G-6 Trop, IV./JG 3, Italy, summer 1943.
Pilot: *Major* Franz Beyer.
Camouflage, upper surfaces: RLM 74/75, lower surfaces: RLM 76.
Each unit of *Pulk Zerstörer* (Gustavs armed with WGr 21 rocket launchers) based in Italy from July to September 1943
were given the task of harassing the Allied bombers from North Africa flying over the peninsula.

THE Me 109G-6 'TROP'

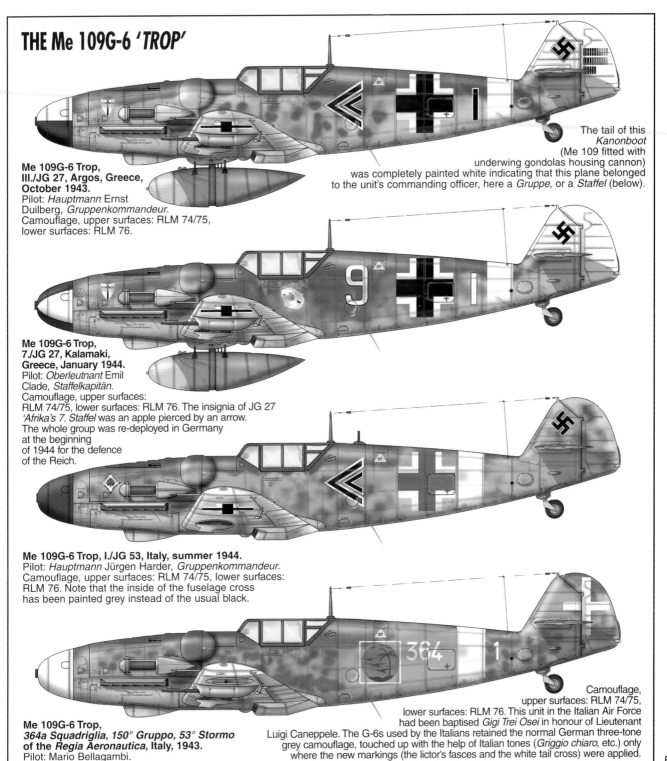

Me 109G-6 Trop,
III./JG 27, Argos, Greece,
October 1943.
Pilot: *Hauptmann* Ernst
Duilberg, *Gruppenkommandeur*.
Camouflage, upper surfaces: RLM 74/75,
lower surfaces: RLM 76.

The tail of this
Kanonboot
(Me 109 fitted with
underwing gondolas housing cannon)
was completely painted white indicating that this plane belonged
to the unit's commanding officer, here a *Gruppe*, or a *Staffel* (below).

Me 109G-6 Trop,
7./JG 27, Kalamaki,
Greece, January 1944.
Pilot: *Oberleutnant* Emil
Clade, *Staffelkapitän*.
Camouflage, upper surfaces:
RLM 74/75, lower surfaces: RLM 76. The insignia of JG 27
'Afrika's 7. Staffel was an apple pierced by an arrow.
The whole group was re-deployed in Germany
at the beginning
of 1944 for the defence
of the Reich.

Me 109G-6 Trop, I./JG 53, Italy, summer 1944.
Pilot: *Hauptmann* Jürgen Harder, *Gruppenkommandeur*.
Camouflage, upper surfaces: RLM 74/75, lower surfaces:
RLM 76. Note that the inside of the fuselage cross
has been painted grey instead of the usual black.

Me 109G-6 Trop,
364a Squadriglia, 150° Gruppo, 53° Stormo
of the *Regia Aeronautica*, Italy, 1943.
Pilot: Mario Bellagambi.

Camouflage,
upper surfaces: RLM 74/75,
lower surfaces: RLM 76. This unit in the Italian Air Force
had been baptised *Gigi Trei Osei* in honour of Lieutenant
Luigi Caneppele. The G-6s used by the Italians retained the normal German three-tone
grey camouflage, touched up with the help of Italian tones (*Griggio chiaro*, etc.) only
where the new markings (the lictor's fasces and the white tail cross) were applied.

THE Me 109G-6 IN ITALIAN SERVICE

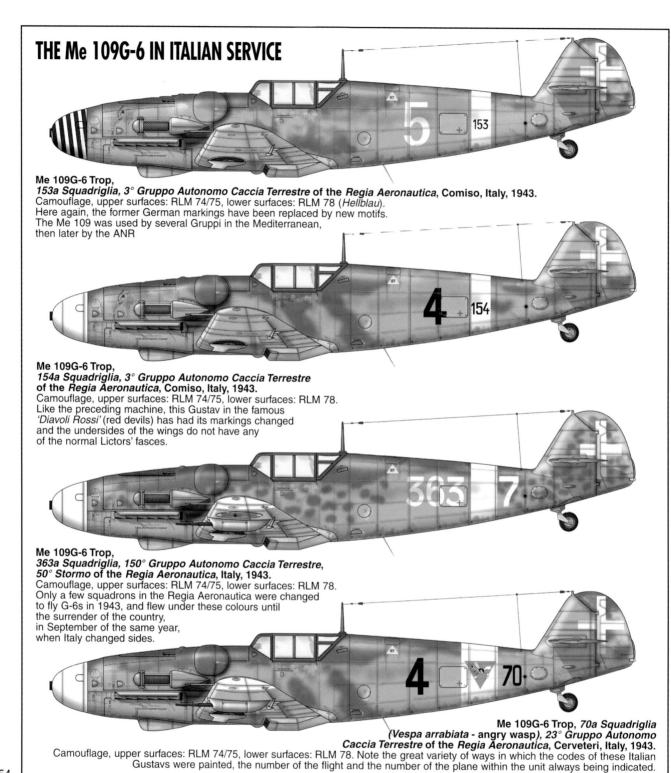

Me 109G-6 Trop,
153a Squadriglia, 3° Gruppo Autonomo Caccia Terrestre of the *Regia Aeronautica*, Comiso, Italy, 1943.
Camouflage, upper surfaces: RLM 74/75, lower surfaces: RLM 78 (*Hellblau*).
Here again, the former German markings have been replaced by new motifs.
The Me 109 was used by several Gruppi in the Mediterranean,
then later by the ANR

Me 109G-6 Trop,
154a Squadriglia, 3° Gruppo Autonomo Caccia Terrestre
of the *Regia Aeronautica*, Comiso, Italy, 1943.
Camouflage, upper surfaces: RLM 74/75, lower surfaces: RLM 78.
Like the preceding machine, this Gustav in the famous
'Diavoli Rossi' (red devils) has had its markings changed
and the undersides of the wings do not have any
of the normal Lictors' fasces.

Me 109G-6 Trop,
363a Squadriglia, 150° Gruppo Autonomo Caccia Terrestre,
50° Stormo of the *Regia Aeronautica*, Italy, 1943.
Camouflage, upper surfaces: RLM 74/75, lower surfaces: RLM 78.
Only a few squadrons in the Regia Aeronautica were changed
to fly G-6s in 1943, and flew under these colours until
the surrender of the country,
in September of the same year,
when Italy changed sides.

Me 109G-6 Trop, *70a Squadriglia*
(Vespa arrabiata - angry wasp), 23° Gruppo Autonomo
Caccia Terrestre of the *Regia Aeronautica*, Cerveteri, Italy, 1943.
Camouflage, upper surfaces: RLM 74/75, lower surfaces: RLM 78. Note the great variety of ways in which the codes of these Italian
Gustavs were painted, the number of the flight and the number of the plane within the unit always being indicated.

THE Me 109G-6 IN FOREIGN COLOURS

From 1942, the Gustav was used by some of the German allies' air forces, particularly Italy, the first country to use the type, in the 15. (*Kroat*)/JG 52. The G-6 was produced in more numbers than any of the other Gustavs and was the most numerous in the foreign air forces also, including Bulgaria and Slovakia, Hungary and Finland where the model was very successful in the hands of, for instance, Eino Juutlainen, who obtained the majority of his kills aboard an Me 109G. Romania turned the Gustavs it had used alongside the Germans against them when it changed sides. Switzerland obtained a dozen G-6s as a ransom, in exchange for an Me 110 night-fighter equipped with 'sensitive' radar systems. These were used until 1947.

Photo © V. Kermorgant

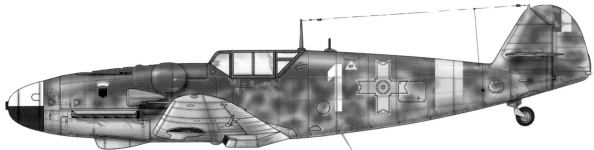

Me 109G-6, *Grupul 9 Vantoare* of the *Aeronautica Regală Română*, Tecuci, Romania, May 1944.
Pilot: *Capitan* Alexandru Serbanescu, commanding the fighter group.
Camouflage, upper surfaces: RLM 74/75, lower surfaces: RLM 76.
Yellow identification markings (RLM 04).
Serbanescu, one of the greatest Romanian aces of WWII
(44 confirmed kills) was shot down by American P-51s
on 18 August 1944, only a few days before his country
changed sides.

Me 109G-6, *Grupul 7 Vanatoare* of the *Aeronautica Regală Română*.
Camouflage, upper surfaces: RLM 74/75, lower surfaces: RLM 76.
Yellow identification markings (RLM 04). This group was equipped with G-6s at the end
of June 1944 to replace the worn-out G-2s. Note the tricolour flag painted on only part of the tail.

55

THE Me 109G-6 IN FOREIGN COLOURS

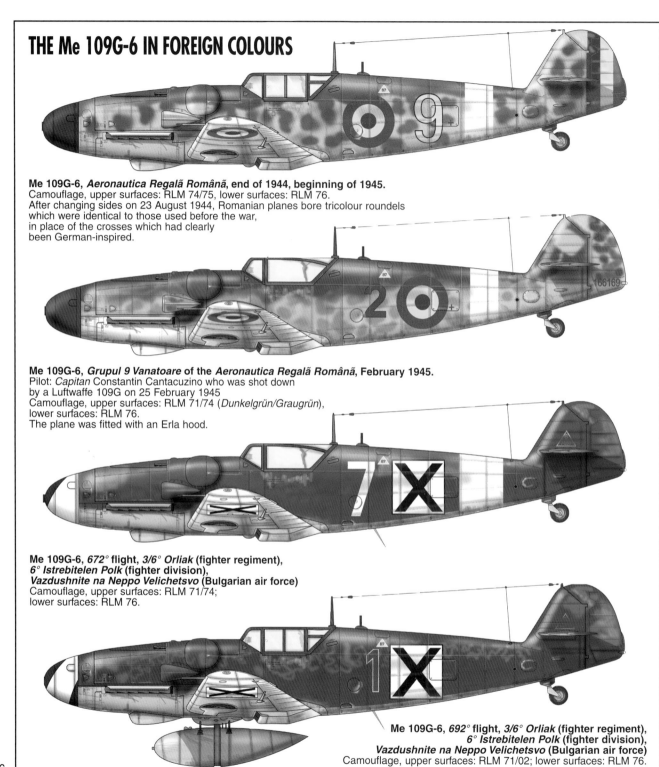

Me 109G-6, *Aeronautica Regalā Românā*, end of 1944, beginning of 1945.
Camouflage, upper surfaces: RLM 74/75, lower surfaces: RLM 76.
After changing sides on 23 August 1944, Romanian planes bore tricolour roundels
which were identical to those used before the war,
in place of the crosses which had clearly
been German-inspired.

Me 109G-6, *Grupul 9 Vanatoare* of the *Aeronautica Regalā Românā*, February 1945.
Pilot: *Capitan* Constantin Cantacuzino who was shot down
by a Luftwaffe 109G on 25 February 1945
Camouflage, upper surfaces: RLM 71/74 (*Dunkelgrün/Graugrün*),
lower surfaces: RLM 76.
The plane was fitted with an Erla hood.

Me 109G-6, *672° flight, 3/6° Orliak* (fighter regiment),
6° *Istrebitelen Polk* (fighter division),
Vazdushnite na Neppo Velichetsvo (Bulgarian air force)
Camouflage, upper surfaces: RLM 71/74;
lower surfaces: RLM 76.

Me 109G-6, *692° flight, 3/6° Orliak* (fighter regiment),
6° *Istrebitelen Polk* (fighter division),
Vazdushnite na Neppo Velichetsvo (Bulgarian air force)
Camouflage, upper surfaces: RLM 71/02; lower surfaces: RLM 76.

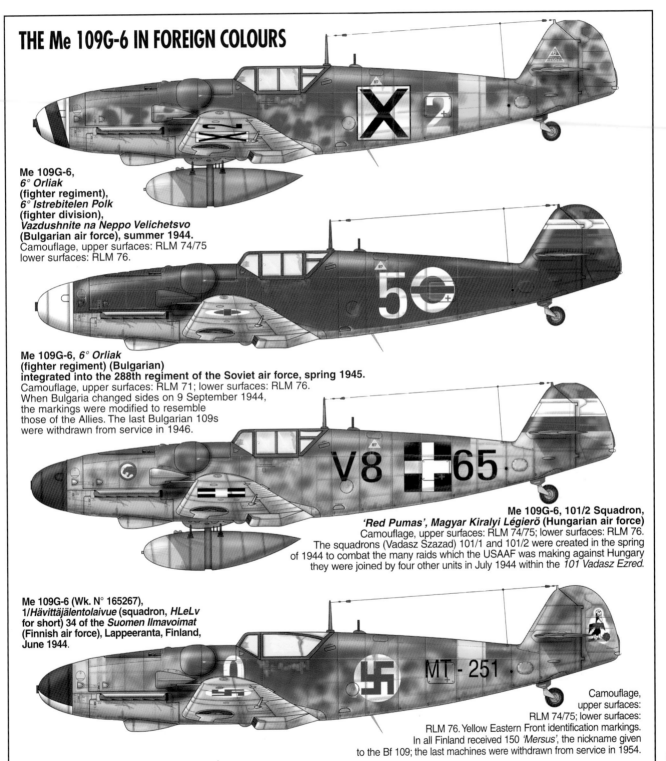

THE Me 109G-6 IN FOREIGN COLOURS

Me 109G-6,
6° Orliak
(fighter regiment),
6° Istrebitelen Polk
(fighter division),
Vazdushnite na Neppo Velichetsvo
(Bulgarian air force), summer 1944.
Camouflage, upper surfaces: RLM 74/75
lower surfaces: RLM 76.

Me 109G-6, *6° Orliak*
(fighter regiment) (Bulgarian)
integrated into the 288th regiment of the Soviet air force, spring 1945.
Camouflage, upper surfaces: RLM 71; lower surfaces: RLM 76.
When Bulgaria changed sides on 9 September 1944,
the markings were modified to resemble
those of the Allies. The last Bulgarian 109s
were withdrawn from service in 1946.

Me 109G-6, 101/2 Squadron,
'Red Pumas', Magyar Kiralyi Légierö (Hungarian air force)
Camouflage, upper surfaces: RLM 74/75; lower surfaces: RLM 76.
The squadrons (Vadasz Szazad) 101/1 and 101/2 were created in the spring
of 1944 to combat the many raids which the USAAF was making against Hungary
they were joined by four other units in July 1944 within the *101 Vadasz Ezred*.

Me 109G-6 (Wk. N° 165267),
1/*Hävittäjälentolaivue* (squadron, *HLeLv*
for short) 34 of the *Suomen Ilmavoimat*
(Finnish air force), Lappeeranta, Finland,
June 1944.

Camouflage,
upper surfaces:
RLM 74/75; lower surfaces:
RLM 76. Yellow Eastern Front identification markings.
In all Finland received 150 *'Mersus'*, the nickname given
to the Bf 109; the last machines were withdrawn from service in 1954.

THE Me 109G-6 IN FOREIGN COLOURS

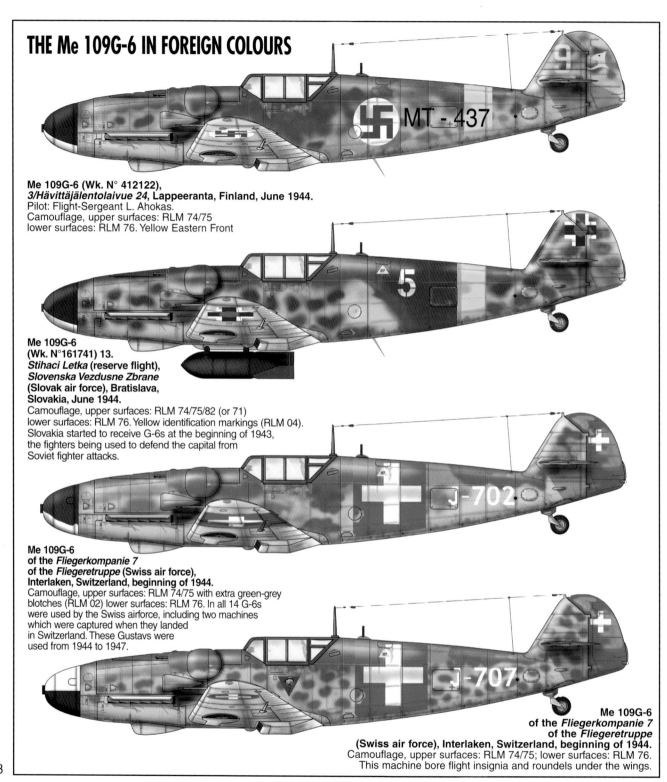

Me 109G-6 (Wk. N° 412122),
***3/Hävittäjälentolaivue 24*, Lappeeranta, Finland, June 1944.**
Pilot: Flight-Sergeant L. Ahokas.
Camouflage, upper surfaces: RLM 74/75
lower surfaces: RLM 76. Yellow Eastern Front

Me 109G-6
(Wk. N°161741) 13.
***Stihaci Letka* (reserve flight),**
Slovenska Vezdusne Zbrane
(Slovak air force), Bratislava,
Slovakia, June 1944.
Camouflage, upper surfaces: RLM 74/75/82 (or 71)
lower surfaces: RLM 76. Yellow identification markings (RLM 04).
Slovakia started to receive G-6s at the beginning of 1943,
the fighters being used to defend the capital from
Soviet fighter attacks.

Me 109G-6
of the *Fliegerkompanie 7*
of the *Fliegeretruppe* (Swiss air force),
Interlaken, Switzerland, beginning of 1944.
Camouflage, upper surfaces: RLM 74/75 with extra green-grey
blotches (RLM 02) lower surfaces: RLM 76. In all 14 G-6s
were used by the Swiss airforce, including two machines
which were captured when they landed
in Switzerland. These Gustavs were
used from 1944 to 1947.

Me 109G-6
of the *Fliegerkompanie 7*
of the *Fliegeretruppe*
(Swiss air force), Interlaken, Switzerland, beginning of 1944.
Camouflage, upper surfaces: RLM 74/75; lower surfaces: RLM 76.
This machine bore flight insignia and roundels under the wings.

Me 109 G-10

Built from October 1944 until the end of the war, the G-10 - the fastest of all the Gustavs - was not much of an improvement on the preceding models; it was rather a cheap and simple means of getting almost the same machine as the K-4 (which was produced in parallel) by converting old airframes. The transformation programme was originally very ambitious envisaging as it did the production of almost 6 000 machines before the month of August. As can be imagined, this target was never reached, G-10 production — the real figure is not known — having reached around 2 600 machines.

Like with the G-14 which preceded it chronologically, there was no standard version of the G-10, as it was produced in a multitude of variants. It was theoretically to have been powered by the new and better DB605D — in fact a DB605AS with higher compression rate and larger cubic capacity. But as it was not immediately available when the first machines started coming off the production line, it was replaced by the DB605AS and this aircraft, almost identical to the G-14/AS, was designated logically G-10/AS.

When the DB605D was finally installed it was very often fitted with the MW50 power boost system; the front part of the engine cowling was modified slightly with two small bumps just under the first exhaust pipe. It also used the wider and deeper Fo 987 oil radiator [n1] [n2]. This modification was not however one of the powerplant's standard features; some G-14/ASs and G-10/ASs equipped in this manner are known to have existed.

As the G-10 resulted from a modification of existing machines, different configurations were bound to be encountered, all depended on the origin of the machines or on the availability of the different elements such as rectangular or tear-drop shaped wing fairings for the large or smaller wheels, long or short tailwheels.

Most G-10s were fitted with the larger tailfin and rudder, although some machines had the smaller tail fin. The Erla hood seems to have been fitted as standard as was the FuG 16zy radio antenna mast fitted under the port wing. The 300-litre drop-tank (*Rüstsatz* R3) was very widely used thereby increasing the fighter's already limited range. It seems that other conversions were envisaged but few, if any were used, except for the R2 which corresponded to the reconnaissance version, equipped with Rb50/30 cameras installed in the fuselage.

This G-10AS was recovered by the Allies almost intact on an airfield near Munich.
(D.R.)

In November 1944, Germany produced a number of planes which were far superior to anything else produced at any other moment of the war; the majority of them were Bf 109s in their different versions. The Luftwaffe's especially dire situation was due to the chronic lack of fuel and to the inexperience of the pilots. At the time, the Me 109 was faster than ever, but it had become heavier and less manoeuvrable and only the aces, and then very few of them, were able to get the most out of it.

When it came into service, the G-10 was the fastest of the all the Me 109s ever built but it was not able however to change the course of the war. Its role was made all the more difficult by the arrival of the P-51 Mustang and the later versions of the Spitfire used to escort the large bomber formations — the German fighters' favourite targets — deep into the heart of the Reich which made the pilot's job all the more dangerous.

Like all the fighters available at the time, the G-10s took part in *Operation Bodenplatte* on 1 January 1945, the last massed attack put up by the Luftwaffe which ended with the loss of allied 400 aircraft; but it was their gallant last stand. The Germans were no longer able to replace their pilot casualties. This was certainly not the case with the opposite side which had far more reserves to draw on.

Specifications - Bf 109G-10

Type
Single-seat fighter

Motorisation
One Daimler-Benz DB 605D liquid-cooled 12-cylinder in-line engine giving 2,000-bhp on take off.

Performances
Max speed: 690 km/h at 7 500 m; 544 kph at sea-level.

Dimensions
Wingspan: 9.92 m
Length: 9.02 m
Height: 3.40 m
Wing area: 16.05m²

Armament
Two MG 131/13 13-mm machine guns with 300 rounds. One MK 108 30-mm canon.

59

THE Me 109G-10 IN THE LUFTWAFFE

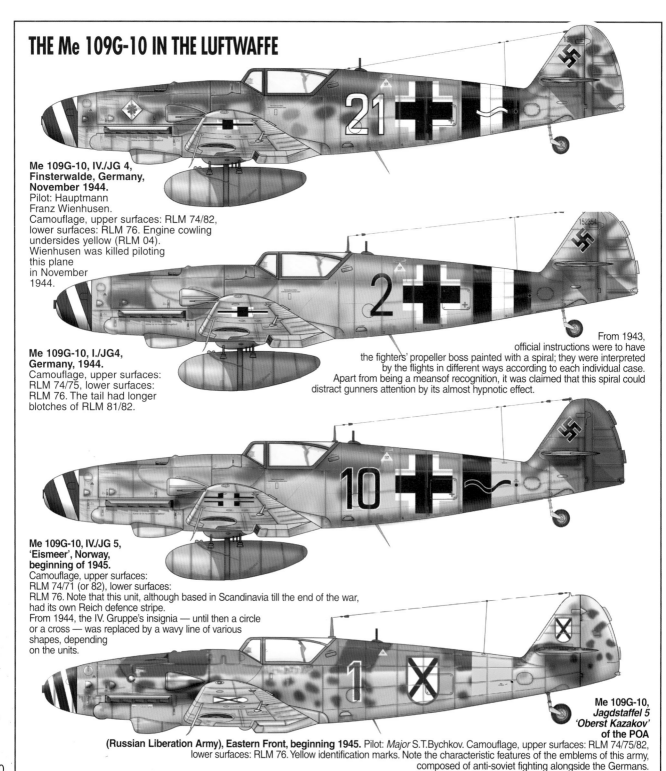

Me 109G-10, IV./JG 4, Finsterwalde, Germany, November 1944.
Pilot: Hauptmann Franz Wienhusen.
Camouflage, upper surfaces: RLM 74/82, lower surfaces: RLM 76. Engine cowling undersides yellow (RLM 04). Wienhusen was killed piloting this plane in November 1944.

Me 109G-10, I./JG4, Germany, 1944.
Camouflage, upper surfaces: RLM 74/75, lower surfaces: RLM 76. The tail had longer blotches of RLM 81/82.

From 1943, official instructions were to have the fighters' propeller boss painted with a spiral; they were interpreted by the flights in different ways according to each individual case. Apart from being a means of recognition, it was claimed that this spiral could distract gunners attention by its almost hypnotic effect.

Me 109G-10, IV./JG 5, 'Eismeer', Norway, beginning of 1945.
Camouflage, upper surfaces: RLM 74/71 (or 82), lower surfaces: RLM 76. Note that this unit, although based in Scandinavia till the end of the war, had its own Reich defence stripe.
From 1944, the IV. Gruppe's insignia — until then a circle or a cross — was replaced by a wavy line of various shapes, depending on the units.

Me 109G-10, Jagdstaffel 5 'Oberst Kazakov' of the POA (Russian Liberation Army), Eastern Front, beginning 1945. Pilot: *Major* S.T.Bychkov. Camouflage, upper surfaces: RLM 74/75/82, lower surfaces: RLM 76. Yellow identification marks. Note the characteristic features of the emblems of this army, composed of anti-soviet fighting alongside the Germans.

THE Me 109G-10 IN THE LUFTWAFFE

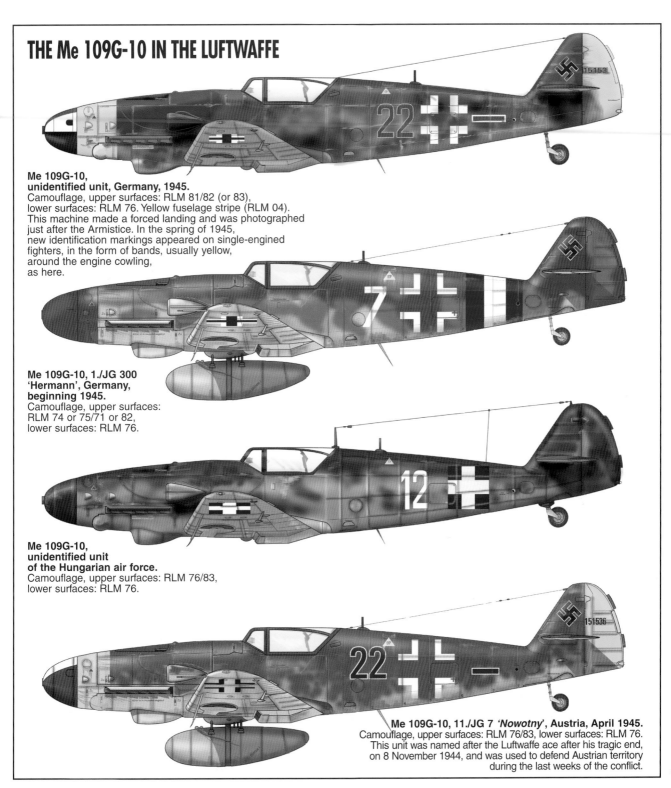

Me 109G-10,
unidentified unit, Germany, 1945.
Camouflage, upper surfaces: RLM 81/82 (or 83),
lower surfaces: RLM 76. Yellow fuselage stripe (RLM 04).
This machine made a forced landing and was photographed
just after the Armistice. In the spring of 1945,
new identification markings appeared on single-engined
fighters, in the form of bands, usually yellow,
around the engine cowling,
as here.

Me 109G-10, 1./JG 300
'Hermann', Germany,
beginning 1945.
Camouflage, upper surfaces:
RLM 74 or 75/71 or 82,
lower surfaces: RLM 76.

Me 109G-10,
unidentified unit
of the Hungarian air force.
Camouflage, upper surfaces: RLM 76/83,
lower surfaces: RLM 76.

Me 109G-10, 11./JG 7 '*Nowotny*', Austria, April 1945.
Camouflage, upper surfaces: RLM 76/83, lower surfaces: RLM 76.
This unit was named after the Luftwaffe ace after his tragic end,
on 8 November 1944, and was used to defend Austrian territory
during the last weeks of the conflict.

THE Me 109G-10 IN THE LUFTWAFFE

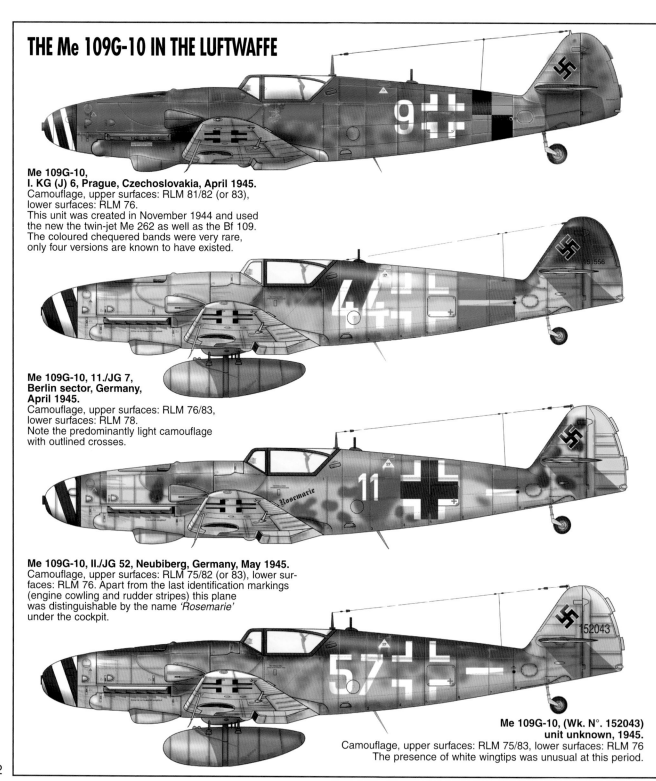

Me 109G-10,
I. KG (J) 6, Prague, Czechoslovakia, April 1945.
Camouflage, upper surfaces: RLM 81/82 (or 83),
lower surfaces: RLM 76.
This unit was created in November 1944 and used
the new the twin-jet Me 262 as well as the Bf 109.
The coloured chequered bands were very rare,
only four versions are known to have existed.

Me 109G-10, 11./JG 7,
Berlin sector, Germany,
April 1945.
Camouflage, upper surfaces: RLM 76/83,
lower surfaces: RLM 78.
Note the predominantly light camouflage
with outlined crosses.

Me 109G-10, II./JG 52, Neubiberg, Germany, May 1945.
Camouflage, upper surfaces: RLM 75/82 (or 83), lower surfaces: RLM 76. Apart from the last identification markings
(engine cowling and rudder stripes) this plane
was distinguishable by the name *'Rosemarie'*
under the cockpit.

Me 109G-10, (Wk. N°. 152043)
unit unknown, 1945.
Camouflage, upper surfaces: RLM 75/83, lower surfaces: RLM 76
The presence of white wingtips was unusual at this period.

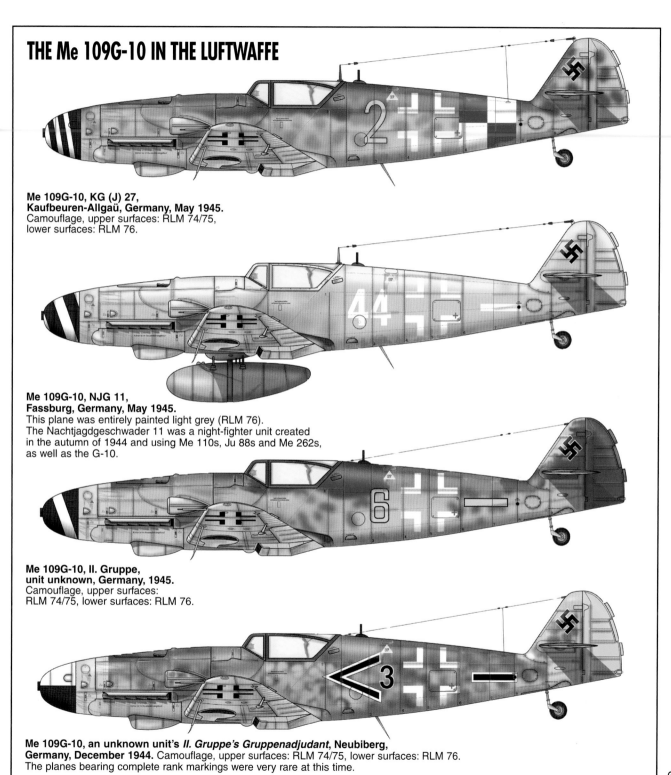

THE Me 109G-10 IN THE LUFTWAFFE

Me 109G-10, KG (J) 27,
Kaufbeuren-Allgaü, Germany, May 1945.
Camouflage, upper surfaces: RLM 74/75,
lower surfaces: RLM 76.

Me 109G-10, NJG 11,
Fassburg, Germany, May 1945.
This plane was entirely painted light grey (RLM 76).
The Nachtjagdgeschwader 11 was a night-fighter unit created
in the autumn of 1944 and using Me 110s, Ju 88s and Me 262s,
as well as the G-10.

Me 109G-10, II. Gruppe,
unit unknown, Germany, 1945.
Camouflage, upper surfaces:
RLM 74/75, lower surfaces: RLM 76.

Me 109G-10, an unknown unit's *II. Gruppe's Gruppenadjudant*, **Neubiberg,**
Germany, December 1944. Camouflage, upper surfaces: RLM 74/75, lower surfaces: RLM 76.
The planes bearing complete rank markings were very rare at this time.

Me 109 G-8, G-12, G-14

The Bf 109G-8 was not properly speaking a real version of the Gustav; it was rather a G-6 specialised in tactical reconnaissance.

Production of this variant began in August 1943 and seems to have continued until the beginning of 1945. Compared with previous variants of the reconnaissance Gustavs, the G-8 carried not only photographic equipment (Rb for *Reihenbildkamera*) with different focal lengths fitted into the fuselage, but also another camera, made by *Robot*, fitted into the leading edge of the port wing, aimed by using the sights. This set up was designed to take photographs from a height of 2 000 metres, but turned out not to be very effective and was removed from the machines to which it had already been fitted and then was simply left out of the machines at the end of the production run.

Basically, the G-8 was nothing but a G-6 whose frames N° 5 and 6 had been reinforced in order to take the cameras, with two shuttered openings inserted on the underside of the fuselage. The radio equipment was also different and the antenna mast was placed further back, on the dorsal ridge at the same level as the camera compartment. Several conversions and modifications were made to this version to give it more power and speed, some machines even dispensing with armament to reduce weight. Put into service in November 1943, about 900 were produced and it became the standard machine for the Tactical reconnaissance group pilots (*Nahaufklärungsgruppen* or *NAGr*) especially the 3./NAGr 13 which operated from the Chartres sector. Two pilots from this unit carried out the first armed reconnaissance flight over the Normandy beaches on the morning of 6 June 1944.

The G-12 was not actually a real version of the Gustav either, i.e. built as such from the outset. To obtain an advanced trainer quickly and cheaply for future fighter pilots, it was decided to get the Gustav cells (G-2, -3,-4 and -6) already in service transformed by maintenance units and not in the factories. A second cockpit was added behind the first one equipped with its own hinged canopy and convex glass in order to afford minimum visibility towards the front. Normally the student was placed in front, but he could however sit behind and practice instrument flying, his canopy in this case being covered. The

This Me 109 G-14 was found intact by the Allies after the war. It still has the fuselage bumps which were a feature of the G-6, from which it was descended. (RR)

G-12 carried therefore almost half the quantity of fuel because the instructor replaced the fuselage reservoir. In order to give the machine more than the resulting thirty minutes' flying time, a ventral fuel tank was very often fitted.

It had been planned to produce 500 two-seaters from the beginning of 1944 in order to answer the Luftwaffe's need for fighter pilots, which was getting increasingly urgent because of the turn events were taking.

Although the number is not actually known, it seems that this figure was never reached. In theory the G-12s dispensed with all armament, but some machines kept at least the engine-mounted machine guns and it is even conceivable that these machines were used as last ditch interceptors during the last hours of the war.

Then it was the G-14 which appeared because the DB 605D engine planned for the G-10 was not available. This new version was to have incorporated all the improvements which had been made to the G-6 previously; the authorities wanted a standard version in order to rationalise the production undertaken by a multitude of sub-contractors. This attempt failed as this new version was itself turned out in a multitude of different variants one for each of the different changes made…. It was a less effective machine than it successors, namely the G-10 and K; nevertheless, the G-14 was produced in large numbers (about 5 500) until the end of the war, serving in most of the units flying 109s.

If the first G-14s were identical to the end-of-production G-6s, with the majority fitted with the Erla hood, as already mentioned, a host of variants very quickly made their appearance (bigger rudder, lengthened tailwheel, bigger wheels with rectangular square upper wing surface blisters, different canon, etc.) including the very radical G—14/AS (about 1 000 produced), recognisable by its bigger oil radiator. Even though this was not systematically installed, the plane was otherwise in all points similar to the G-6/AS.

THE Me 109G-12 IN THE LUFTWAFFE

Me 109G-12, JG 101, Pau, France.
Camouflage, upper surfaces: RLM 74/75, lower surfaces: RLM 76.
The factory code (*Stammkennzeichen*) was still visible under the fuselage stripe.
This two-seat version was made from a G-2. JG 101 was a fighter pilot training unit, based in France,
and used Arado 96s, its G-12s and even some D.520s.

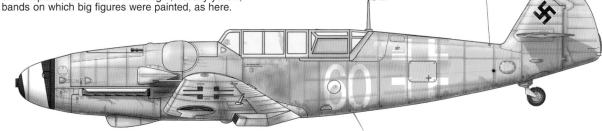

Me 109G-12, 5./JG 108, (ex-I./JG 107), Börgönd, Hungary,
Camouflage, upper surfaces: RLM 74/75, lower surfaces: RLM 76.
Yellow identification markings (RLM 04). This two-seater was made from a G-4.
Originally the fighter training units (*Jagdgeschwaderschulen*) kept their factory code,
often replaced afterwards with bright, usually yellow,
bands on which big figures were painted, as here.

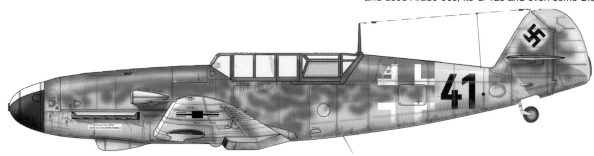

Me 109G-12, unidentified training school
Camouflage completely light grey: RLM 76.
As the bumps on the engine cowling seem to indicate,
this was in fact a G-6 transformed into a two-seater,
by adding another cockpit.

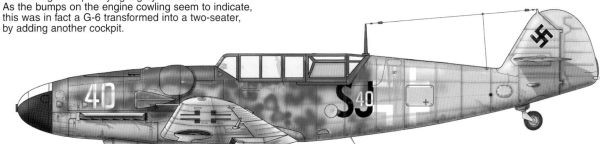

Me 109G-12, I./JG 104.
Camouflage, upper surfaces: RLM 74/75, lower surfaces: RLM 76.
This one was also derived from a G-6. The rear of the plane has been changed from frame n° 4 as the different colour reveals.
The individual number was repeated twice whereas the factory code can be partially seen in front of the fuselage cross.

THE Me 109G-14 IN THE LUFTWAFFE

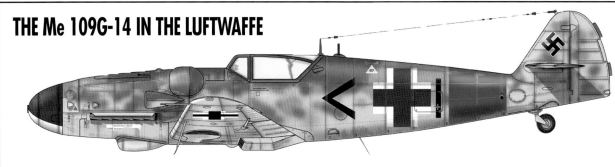

Me 109G-14, III./JG 27, Germany, summer 1944.
Camouflage, upper surfaces: RLM 74/75,
lower surfaces: RLM 76.

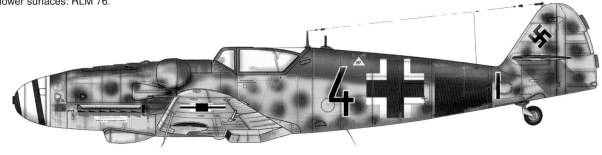

Me 109G-14, 12./JG 53, Operation *'Bodenplatte'*, on 1 January 1945.
Camouflage, upper surfaces: RLM 81/82, lower surfaces: RLM 76.
Apart from its black Reich defence stripe,
this unusually camouflaged plane still had a yellow engine cowling (RLM 04)
and the propeller boss spiral was anti-clockwise compared with the original,
the white stripe being the wider.

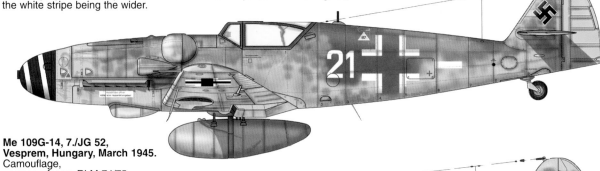

Me 109G-14, 7./JG 52,
Vesprem, Hungary, March 1945.
Camouflage,
upper surfaces: RLM 74/75,
lower surfaces: RLM 76.

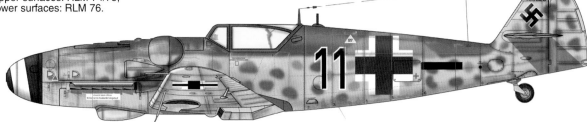

Me 109G-14, (Wk. N° 460570), unit unknown.
Camouflage, upper surfaces: RLM 74/75,
lower surfaces and flanks: RLM 76.

THE Me 109G-14 IN THE LUFTWAFFE

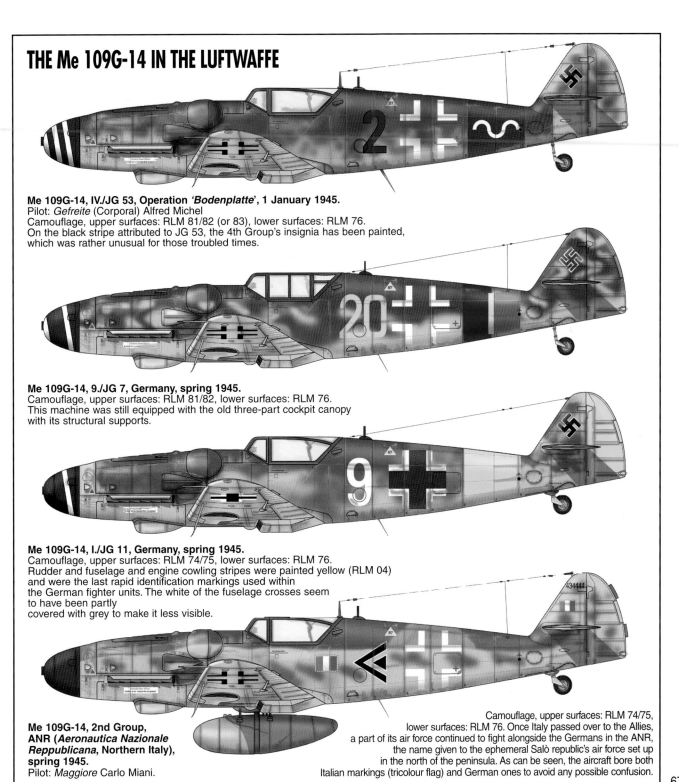

Me 109G-14, IV./JG 53, Operation 'Bodenplatte', 1 January 1945.
Pilot: *Gefreite* (Corporal) Alfred Michel
Camouflage, upper surfaces: RLM 81/82 (or 83), lower surfaces: RLM 76.
On the black stripe attributed to JG 53, the 4th Group's insignia has been painted,
which was rather unusual for those troubled times.

Me 109G-14, 9./JG 7, Germany, spring 1945.
Camouflage, upper surfaces: RLM 81/82, lower surfaces: RLM 76.
This machine was still equipped with the old three-part cockpit canopy
with its structural supports.

Me 109G-14, I./JG 11, Germany, spring 1945.
Camouflage, upper surfaces: RLM 74/75, lower surfaces: RLM 76.
Rudder and fuselage and engine cowling stripes were painted yellow (RLM 04)
and were the last rapid identification markings used within
the German fighter units. The white of the fuselage crosses seem
to have been partly
covered with grey to make it less visible.

**Me 109G-14, 2nd Group,
ANR (*Aeronautica Nazionale
Reppublicana*, Northern Italy),
spring 1945.**
Pilot: *Maggiore* Carlo Miani.

Camouflage, upper surfaces: RLM 74/75,
lower surfaces: RLM 76. Once Italy passed over to the Allies,
a part of its air force continued to fight alongside the Germans in the ANR,
the name given to the ephemeral Salò republic's air force set up
in the north of the peninsula. As can be seen, the aircraft bore both
Italian markings (tricolour flag) and German ones to avoid any possible confusion.

REICH DEFENCE BANDS (REICHSVERTEIDIGUNG)

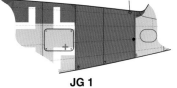

JG 1
JG 300 début 1945

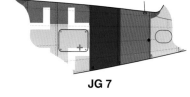

JG 7

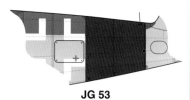

JG 53

JG 2

JG 11

JG 54

JG 3

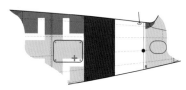

JG 26

JG 77

JG 4

JG 27

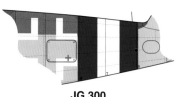

JG 300
(début 1945)

JG 5

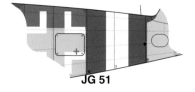

JG 51

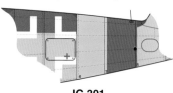

JG 301

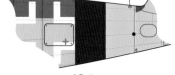

JG 6

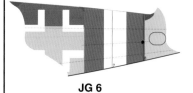

JG 52

From the middle of 1943, German fighters were increasingly used against Allied bombing raids, and needed a rapid-recognition system urgently. At first, the rudders on all fighters taking part in the *Reichsverteidigung* (Defence of the Reich) were painted white; then in January 1944, coloured bands appeared around the rear part of the planes' fuselages. The initial system, using a single-coloured band was quickly replaced by another combining at most two colours, in two or three equal stripes over a total width of 90 cms; an official document dating from February 1945 gives 17 different variants. Because of the situation, these markings were not necessarily applied to all the machines within the same unit, some Jagdgeschwadern not even bearing any of the markings which had been attributed to them.

THE Me 109 K for *KARL*

Planned to replace the G-5 on the production lines, the Bf 109K (or *'Karl'*) was originally to have been fitted with a pressurised cockpit. It was the German authorities' last ditch attempt to rationalise the 109's production programme, following the failure with the G-14 and G-10. It was designed around the new DB605DM rated at 2 000bhp on take-off and deliveries started in October 1944, i.e. before the G-10 which it resembled like two peas in a pod, particularly when the latter's old DB605 AS engine was fitted. In this case only the serial number enabled one to tell the difference.

Although a pre-production series of K-0 powered by the DB605DB without the MW50 power boost system was brought out, the first variants which had been planned (K-1 pressurised, K-2 standard, and K-3 reconnaissance) were abandoned before even being made. (only one K-2 was perhaps built, but it never flew) and it was therefore the K-4 logically which was produced in any numbers. This last version, officially called a 'light fighter' in November 1944 used all the improvements made to the G-10: 'Erla' hood with reduced structural supports, larger tailfin, lengthened tailwheel, bigger oil radiator, wider propeller blades, bigger tyres (meaning rectangular blisters on the wing upper surfaces,) and finally the MK 108 or 103 canon.

In theory the differences with the very last Gustavs can be summarised by the circular radio antenna on the back moved back one frame, the access panel for the radio brought forward one frame and put slightly higher up, ailerons fitted with trim tabs and extra undercarriage doors which were often removed during operations.

The official programme planned a production run of 12 000 K-4s between July 1944 and… March 1946. This figure was obviously never reached and even if the exact number of Karls which came off the production lines will never be known, it does seem that 1 700 were produced.

The K-4s were delivered to Luftwaffe fighter units during the last months of the war and were used together with the G-10s

Me 109 K-4 in II./ JG 3 photographed in the spring of 1945. On the rear fuselage the last part of the hand-painted serial number can still be seen.
(RR)

and G-14s. Because of the worsening situation, the following variants never got past the prototype stage, even if they were built.

Thus the K-6 fitted with two MK 108 cannon in the wings as well as the standard armament was only tested, whereas the reconnaissance K-8, the K-10 fighter and the two-seat K-12 remained where they were, on the drawing board.

The very last variant and the *'last of the 109s'*, the high altitude K-14 fighter, was to have been powered by the DB605L giving it a maximum speed of 730 kph at 11 500 m, nearly 200kph faster than an Emil and only four years older.

Specifications - 109K-4

Type
Single-seat fighter.

Motorisation
One Daimler-Benz DB 605D liquid-cooled 12-cylinder in-line engine rated at 2 000-bhp on take-off.

Dimensions
Wingspan: 9.92 m
Length: 9.02 m
Height: 3.40 m
Wing area: 16.05 m_
Weight (empty): 2 700kg

Weight (take-off, loaded):
3 386kg

Performances
Max. Speed: 727kph at 6 000m
Max. Ceiling: 12 500 m

Armament
Two MG 131/13 13-mm machine guns with 300rpg.
One MG 151/20 20-mm canon with 65 rounds (or one 108 30-mm canon.)

69

THE Me 109K IN THE LUFTWAFFE

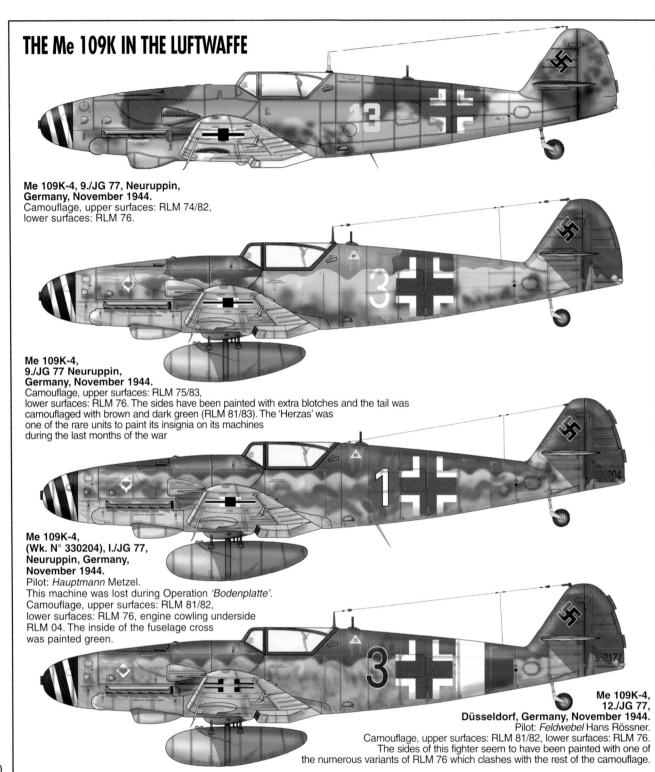

**Me 109K-4, 9./JG 77, Neuruppin,
Germany, November 1944.**
Camouflage, upper surfaces: RLM 74/82,
lower surfaces: RLM 76.

**Me 109K-4,
9./JG 77 Neuruppin,
Germany, November 1944.**
Camouflage, upper surfaces: RLM 75/83,
lower surfaces: RLM 76. The sides have been painted with extra blotches and the tail was
camouflaged with brown and dark green (RLM 81/83). The 'Herzas' was
one of the rare units to paint its insignia on its machines
during the last months of the war

**Me 109K-4,
(Wk. N° 330204), I./JG 77,
Neuruppin, Germany,
November 1944.**
Pilot: *Hauptmann* Metzel.
This machine was lost during Operation *'Bodenplatte'*.
Camouflage, upper surfaces: RLM 81/82,
lower surfaces: RLM 76, engine cowling underside
RLM 04. The inside of the fuselage cross
was painted green.

**Me 109K-4,
12./JG 77,
Düsseldorf, Germany, November 1944.**
Pilot: *Feldwebel* Hans Rössner.
Camouflage, upper surfaces: RLM 81/82, lower surfaces: RLM 76.
The sides of this fighter seem to have been painted with one of
the numerous variants of RLM 76 which clashes with the rest of the camouflage.

THE Me 109K IN THE LUFTWAFFE

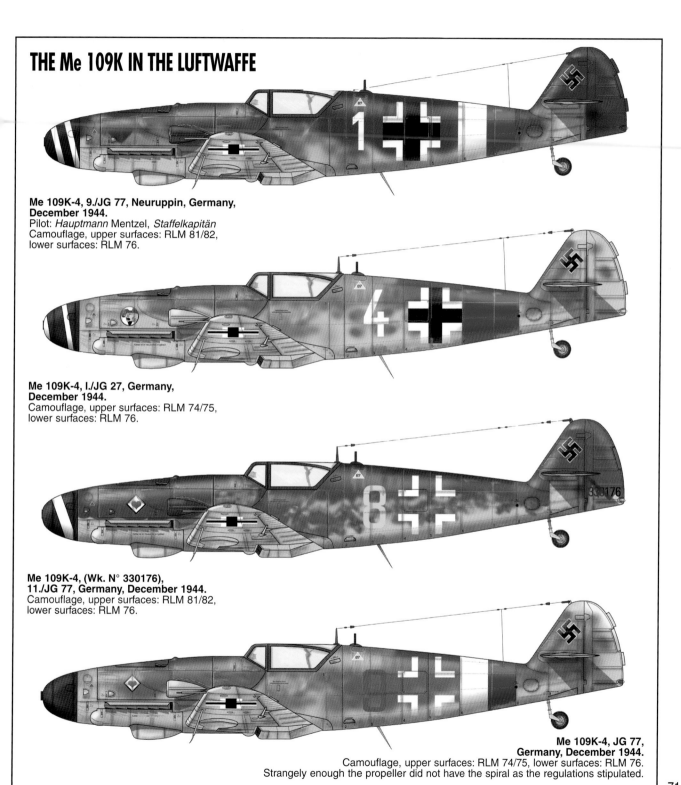

Me 109K-4, 9./JG 77, Neuruppin, Germany, December 1944.
Pilot: *Hauptmann* Mentzel, *Staffelkapitän*
Camouflage, upper surfaces: RLM 81/82, lower surfaces: RLM 76.

Me 109K-4, I./JG 27, Germany, December 1944.
Camouflage, upper surfaces: RLM 74/75, lower surfaces: RLM 76.

Me 109K-4, (Wk. N° 330176), 11./JG 77, Germany, December 1944.
Camouflage, upper surfaces: RLM 81/82, lower surfaces: RLM 76.

Me 109K-4, JG 77, Germany, December 1944.
Camouflage, upper surfaces: RLM 74/75, lower surfaces: RLM 76.
Strangely enough the propeller did not have the spiral as the regulations stipulated.

THE Me 109K IN THE LUFTWAFFE

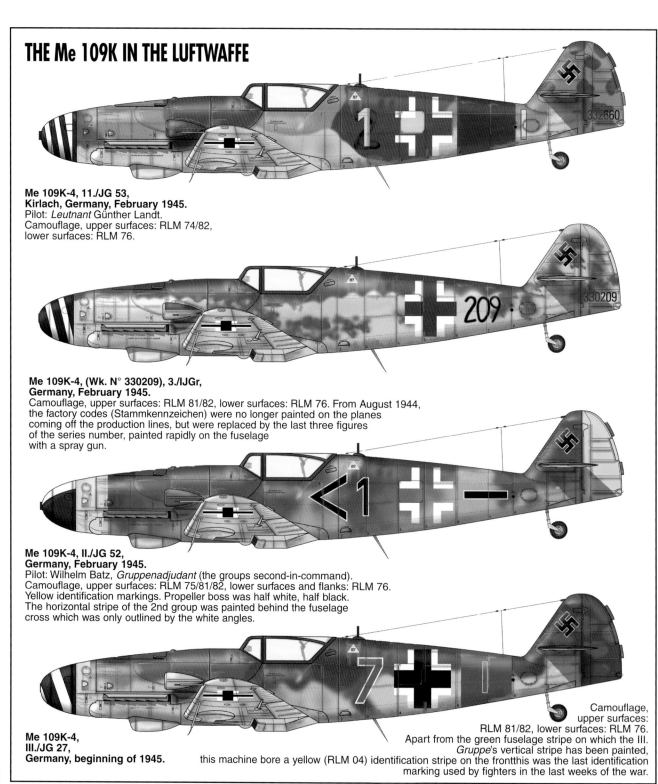

Me 109K-4, 11./JG 53,
Kirlach, Germany, February 1945.
Pilot: *Leutnant* Günther Landt.
Camouflage, upper surfaces: RLM 74/82,
lower surfaces: RLM 76.

Me 109K-4, (Wk. N° 330209), 3./IJGr,
Germany, February 1945.
Camouflage, upper surfaces: RLM 81/82, lower surfaces: RLM 76. From August 1944,
the factory codes (Stammkennzeichen) were no longer painted on the planes
coming off the production lines, but were replaced by the last three figures
of the series number, painted rapidly on the fuselage
with a spray gun.

Me 109K-4, II./JG 52,
Germany, February 1945.
Pilot: Wilhelm Batz, *Gruppenadjudant* (the groups second-in-command).
Camouflage, upper surfaces: RLM 75/81/82, lower surfaces and flanks: RLM 76.
Yellow identification markings. Propeller boss was half white, half black.
The horizontal stripe of the 2nd group was painted behind the fuselage
cross which was only outlined by the white angles.

Me 109K-4,
III./JG 27,
Germany, beginning of 1945.

Camouflage,
upper surfaces:
RLM 81/82, lower surfaces: RLM 76.
Apart from the green fuselage stripe on which the III.
Gruppe's vertical stripe has been painted,
this machine bore a yellow (RLM 04) identification stripe on the frontthis was the last identification
marking used by fighters in the last weeks of the war.

THE Me 109K IN THE LUFTWAFFE

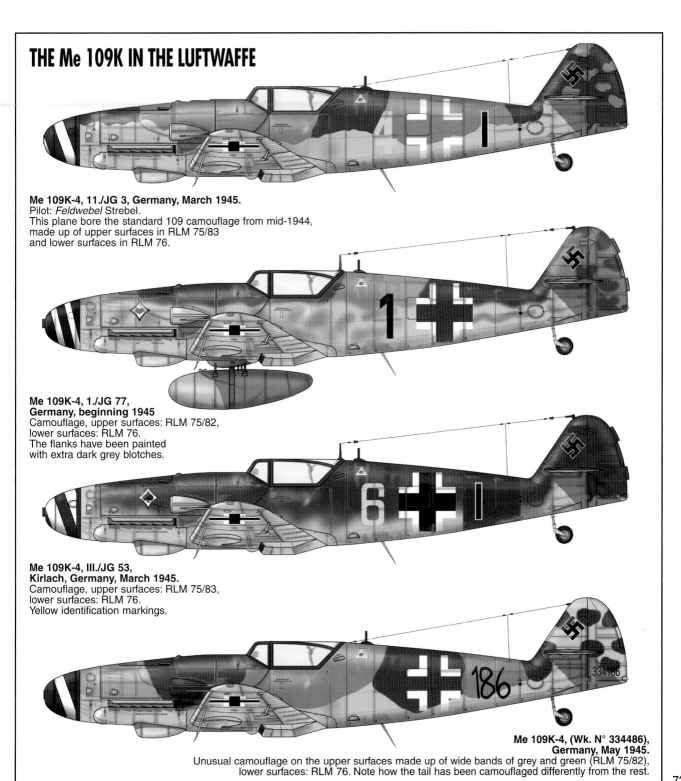

Me 109K-4, 11./JG 3, Germany, March 1945.
Pilot: *Feldwebel* Strebel.
This plane bore the standard 109 camouflage from mid-1944,
made up of upper surfaces in RLM 75/83
and lower surfaces in RLM 76.

**Me 109K-4, 1./JG 77,
Germany, beginning 1945**
Camouflage, upper surfaces: RLM 75/82,
lower surfaces: RLM 76.
The flanks have been painted
with extra dark grey blotches.

**Me 109K-4, III./JG 53,
Kirlach, Germany, March 1945.**
Camouflage, upper surfaces: RLM 75/83,
lower surfaces: RLM 76.
Yellow identification markings.

**Me 109K-4, (Wk. N° 334486),
Germany, May 1945.**
Unusual camouflage on the upper surfaces made up of wide bands of grey and green (RLM 75/82),
lower surfaces: RLM 76. Note how the tail has been camouflaged differently from the rest.

THE Me 109K IN THE LUFTWAFFE

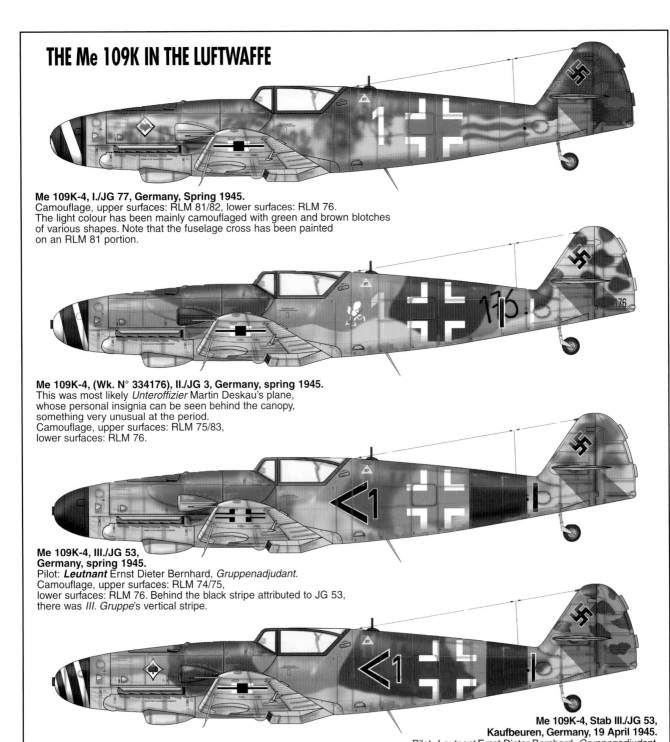

Me 109K-4, I./JG 77, Germany, Spring 1945.
Camouflage, upper surfaces: RLM 81/82, lower surfaces: RLM 76.
The light colour has been mainly camouflaged with green and brown blotches
of various shapes. Note that the fuselage cross has been painted
on an RLM 81 portion.

Me 109K-4, (Wk. N° 334176), II./JG 3, Germany, spring 1945.
This was most likely *Unteroffizier* Martin Deskau's plane,
whose personal insignia can be seen behind the canopy,
something very unusual at the period.
Camouflage, upper surfaces: RLM 75/83,
lower surfaces: RLM 76.

**Me 109K-4, III./JG 53,
Germany, spring 1945.**
Pilot: ***Leutnant*** Ernst Dieter Bernhard, *Gruppenadjudant*.
Camouflage, upper surfaces: RLM 74/75,
lower surfaces: RLM 76. Behind the black stripe attributed to JG 53,
there was *III. Gruppe*'s vertical stripe.

**Me 109K-4, Stab III./JG 53,
Kaufbeuren, Germany, 19 April 1945.**
Pilot: *Leutnant* Ernst Dieter Bernhard, *Gruppenadjudant*.
Camouflage, upper surfaces: RLM 75/83 with extra blotches of RLM 81, lower surfaces: RLM 76. The undersides of the engine cowling
were RLM 04 yellow. Maybe it is the same machine as the previous one but interpreted differently from another photograph.

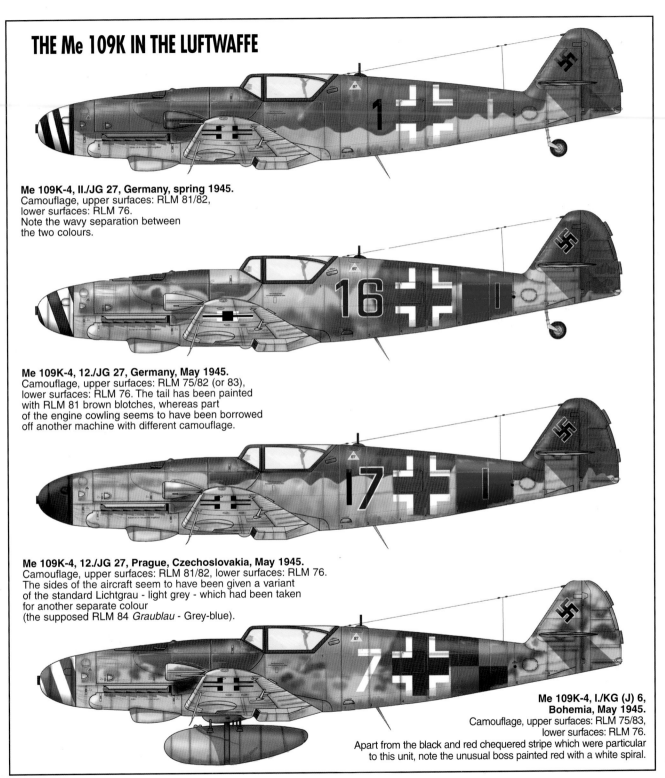

THE Me 109K IN THE LUFTWAFFE

Me 109K-4, II./JG 27, Germany, spring 1945.
Camouflage, upper surfaces: RLM 81/82,
lower surfaces: RLM 76.
Note the wavy separation between
the two colours.

Me 109K-4, 12./JG 27, Germany, May 1945.
Camouflage, upper surfaces: RLM 75/82 (or 83),
lower surfaces: RLM 76. The tail has been painted
with RLM 81 brown blotches, whereas part
of the engine cowling seems to have been borrowed
off another machine with different camouflage.

Me 109K-4, 12./JG 27, Prague, Czechoslovakia, May 1945.
Camouflage, upper surfaces: RLM 81/82, lower surfaces: RLM 76.
The sides of the aircraft seem to have been given a variant
of the standard Lichtgrau - light grey - which had been taken
for another separate colour
(the supposed RLM 84 *Graublau* - Grey-blue).

**Me 109K-4, I./KG (J) 6,
Bohemia, May 1945.**
Camouflage, upper surfaces: RLM 75/83,
lower surfaces: RLM 76.
Apart from the black and red chequered stripe which were particular
to this unit, note the unusual boss painted red with a white spiral.

THE Me 109K IN THE LUFTWAFFE

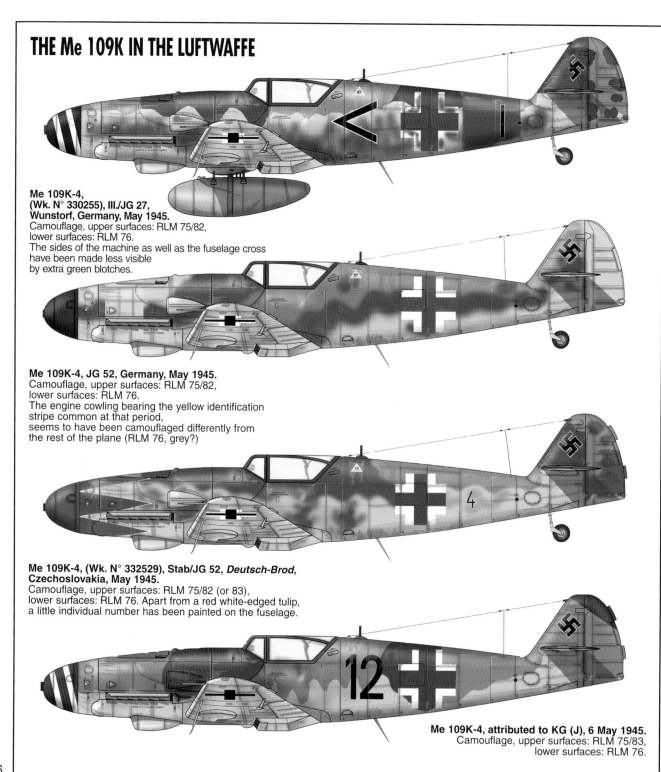

Me 109K-4,
(Wk. N° 330255), III./JG 27,
Wunstorf, Germany, May 1945.
Camouflage, upper surfaces: RLM 75/82,
lower surfaces: RLM 76.
The sides of the machine as well as the fuselage cross
have been made less visible
by extra green blotches.

Me 109K-4, JG 52, Germany, May 1945.
Camouflage, upper surfaces: RLM 75/82,
lower surfaces: RLM 76.
The engine cowling bearing the yellow identification
stripe common at that period,
seems to have been camouflaged differently from
the rest of the plane (RLM 76, grey?)

Me 109K-4, (Wk. N° 332529), Stab/JG 52, *Deutsch-Brod*,
Czechoslovakia, May 1945.
Camouflage, upper surfaces: RLM 75/82 (or 83),
lower surfaces: RLM 76. Apart from a red white-edged tulip,
a little individual number has been painted on the fuselage.

Me 109K-4, attributed to KG (J), 6 May 1945.
Camouflage, upper surfaces: RLM 75/83,
lower surfaces: RLM 76.

THE Me 109K IN THE LUFTWAFFE

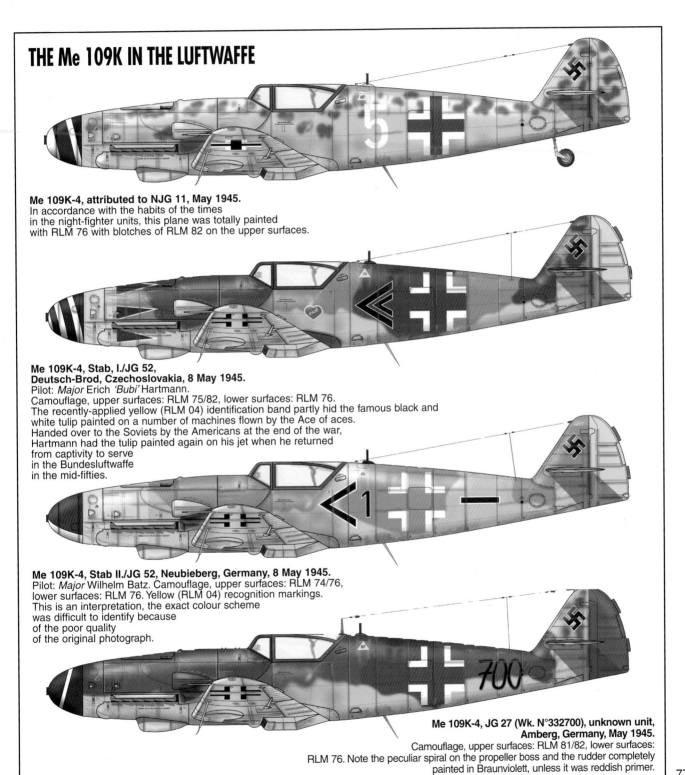

Me 109K-4, attributed to NJG 11, May 1945.
In accordance with the habits of the times
in the night-fighter units, this plane was totally painted
with RLM 76 with blotches of RLM 82 on the upper surfaces.

Me 109K-4, Stab, I./JG 52,
Deutsch-Brod, Czechoslovakia, 8 May 1945.
Pilot: *Major* Erich *'Bubi'* Hartmann.
Camouflage, upper surfaces: RLM 75/82, lower surfaces: RLM 76.
The recently-applied yellow (RLM 04) identification band partly hid the famous black and
white tulip painted on a number of machines flown by the Ace of aces.
Handed over to the Soviets by the Americans at the end of the war,
Hartmann had the tulip painted again on his jet when he returned
from captivity to serve
in the Bundesluftwaffe
in the mid-fifties.

Me 109K-4, Stab II./JG 52, Neubieberg, Germany, 8 May 1945.
Pilot: *Major* Wilhelm Batz. Camouflage, upper surfaces: RLM 74/76,
lower surfaces: RLM 76. Yellow (RLM 04) recognition markings.
This is an interpretation, the exact colour scheme
was difficult to identify because
of the poor quality
of the original photograph.

Me 109K-4, JG 27 (Wk. N°332700), unknown unit,
Amberg, Germany, May 1945.
Camouflage, upper surfaces: RLM 81/82, lower surfaces:
RLM 76. Note the peculiar spiral on the propeller boss and the rudder completely
painted in Braunviolett, unless it was reddish primer.

THE DERIVATIVES of the Bf 109

The long series of Bf 109s did not finish with the *'Karl'*. In fact, even if the later versions (the J, made in Spain under licence; the L powered by a Jumo 213E enabling it to reach 760 kph and equipped with blown flaps making it more manoeuvrable a lower speeds; the twin jet TL planned to reach 850 kph with its two Jumos; not to forget its distant cousins the 209 and 309) remained mere projects - the letter *'I'* was not used of course - Willy Messerschmitt's little fighter continued after the war in various and sometimes rather unexpected guises.

When they were retired from service, many *Buchons* were bought by private collectors who transformed them into Luftwaffe Me 109s, as in this photograph.
(© F. Lert)

Before the end of the conflict, several G-12s and G-14s had been built at the Avia factory, near Prague in Czechoslovakia, leaving a large stock of spare parts after the fall of the Third Reich. A re-equipment programme aimed at rearming the Czech air force with these machines was planned and thus twenty or so G-14s, re-designated S-99 and two CS-99 two-seaters were completed before a fire destroyed the stock of DB605AS engines at the end of 1945. The airframe had to be modified so that the Jumo 211F and H engines originally destined for the He 111s twin-engined bomber and available in great numbers could be fitted. This modification meant redesigning the whole of the front part of the machine (cowling, boss and propeller), which was re-designated S-199. In fact this modification affected the machine's performance because the engine was both heavier and less powerful; moreover the VS-11 propeller, bigger than the original one, generated greater torque which the unchanged wing surface could not compensate for.

Delivered in February 1948 and built until 1949, 500 machines of the new fighter, called *'Mezek'* (Mule) by its pilots — which gives a good idea of its performance — were produced (of which about sixty were S.199 two-seaters). 25 were sold to the young state of Israel which used them during its first war of independence. Like their Czech counterparts the Israeli pilots never appreciated the fighter which was still difficult to handle especially when landing and taking off; it was withdrawn from service a year later and replaced by the Spitfire and Mustang P-51 which were very much better, but not before having scored some kills among which an Egyptian C-47.

The other country where the Bf 109 continued its career was Spain where in 1937 the *Ejercito del Aire* was the first to buy the fighter. It received 25 109G-2s which it was to have built under licence under the designation Bf 109J. The airframes never received the original power-plants so CASA which had in the meantime taken over Hispano-Suiza fitted a Hispano-Suiza HS 12Z 89 into the plane which was given the designation HA 1109-J1L. 200 machines were originally planned. But in 1951, the engines were not available in sufficient numbers and were replaced by HS 12Z 17 which were just as powerful but made in France; the new fighter became the HA-1109-K and in its armed version (20 mm cannon in the wings and rockets) the HA-1112-K1L. In all 69 machines were produced with a Hispano-Suiza engine in Spain among which the HA-1109-J built with airframes which had come from Germany.

In 1949, with airframe production easily overtaking that of engines and the aircraft not living up to expectations, a new power-plant was sought for the airframes piling up in the factory. Eventually in 1953, quite ironically, the Spanish Authorities chose the Rolls-Royce Merlin which had powered the Spitfire and the Mustang. It drove a Rotol four-blade propeller. The first plane in this new series flew at the end of 1954 and the definitive version designated HA-1112-M1L (C.4K for the military) and nicknamed *'Buchon'* (Pigeon - because of its tubby front) was armed with rocket-launchers and cannon in the wings. These machines were for ground-attack and for converting pilots to aircraft with higher performance both in Spain and in its possessions in North Africa alongside the HA-1112-M4L two-seaters until November 1965 when the last unit flying the machine was disbanded.

But the *Buchon*'s career was not over for all that. Indeed in 1968 it became a film star, twenty or so of them being bought by the producers of the film *'the Battle of Britain'* who used them to play Bf 109Es together with the B.2H1, the Spanish version of the Heinkel He 111. This appearance was followed by others, the *Buchon* still being a joy for collectors; it enables them to represent — albeit rather vaguely — the Bf 109, even though the surviving machines can now be counted only on the fingers of one hand.

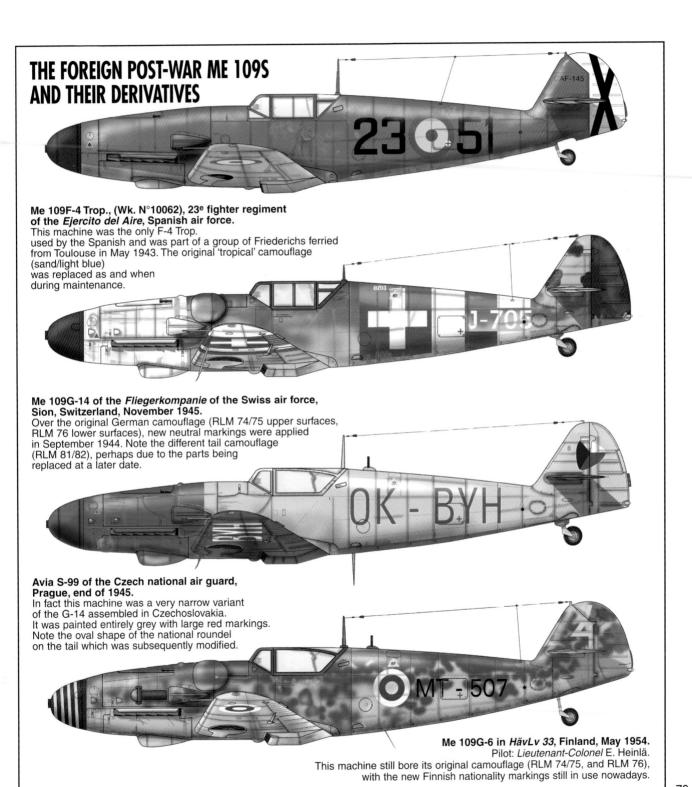

THE FOREIGN POST-WAR ME 109S AND THEIR DERIVATIVES

Me 109F-4 Trop., (Wk. N°10062), 23e fighter regiment of the *Ejercito del Aire*, Spanish air force.
This machine was the only F-4 Trop.
used by the Spanish and was part of a group of Friederichs ferried from Toulouse in May 1943. The original 'tropical' camouflage (sand/light blue)
was replaced as and when
during maintenance.

Me 109G-14 of the *Fliegerkompanie* of the Swiss air force, Sion, Switzerland, November 1945.
Over the original German camouflage (RLM 74/75 upper surfaces, RLM 76 lower surfaces), new neutral markings were applied
in September 1944. Note the different tail camouflage
(RLM 81/82), perhaps due to the parts being
replaced at a later date.

Avia S-99 of the Czech national air guard, Prague, end of 1945.
In fact this machine was a very narrow variant
of the G-14 assembled in Czechoslovakia.
It was painted entirely grey with large red markings.
Note the oval shape of the national roundel
on the tail which was subsequently modified.

Me 109G-6 in *HävLv 33*, Finland, May 1954.
Pilot: *Lieutenant-Colonel* E. Heinlä.
This machine still bore its original camouflage (RLM 74/75, and RLM 76),
with the new Finnish nationality markings still in use nowadays.

THE FOREIGN POST-WAR ME 109S AND THEIR DERIVATIVES

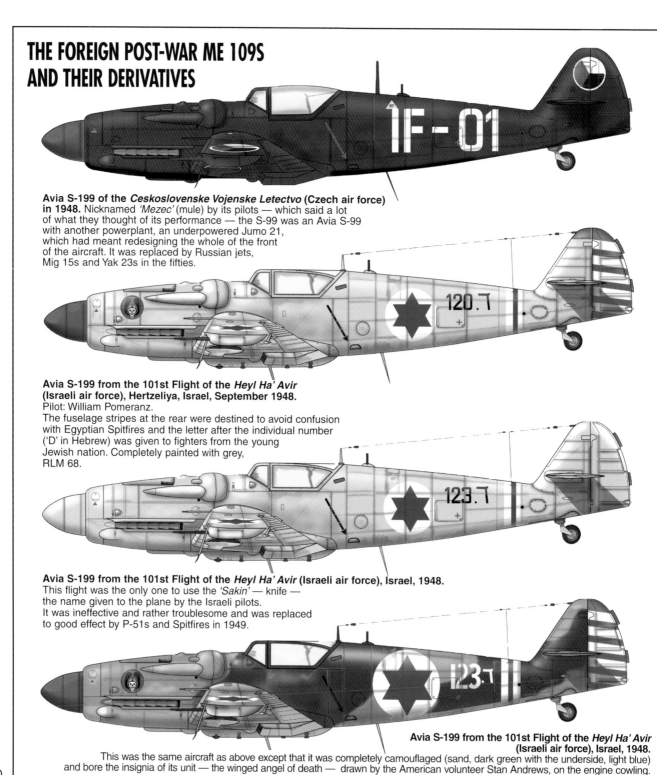

Avia S-199 of the *Ceskoslovenske Vojenske Letectvo* (Czech air force) in 1948. Nicknamed *'Mezec'* (mule) by its pilots — which said a lot of what they thought of its performance — the S-99 was an Avia S-99 with another powerplant, an underpowered Jumo 21, which had meant redesigning the whole of the front of the aircraft. It was replaced by Russian jets, Mig 15s and Yak 23s in the fifties.

Avia S-199 from the 101st Flight of the *Heyl Ha' Avir* (Israeli air force), Hertzeliya, Israel, September 1948.
Pilot: William Pomeranz.
The fuselage stripes at the rear were destined to avoid confusion with Egyptian Spitfires and the letter after the individual number ('D' in Hebrew) was given to fighters from the young Jewish nation. Completely painted with grey, RLM 68.

Avia S-199 from the 101st Flight of the *Heyl Ha' Avir* (Israeli air force), Israel, 1948.
This flight was the only one to use the *'Sakin'* — knife — the name given to the plane by the Israeli pilots.
It was ineffective and rather troublesome and was replaced to good effect by P-51s and Spitfires in 1949.

Avia S-199 from the 101st Flight of the *Heyl Ha' Avir* (Israeli air force), Israel, 1948.
This was the same aircraft as above except that it was completely camouflaged (sand, dark green with the underside, light blue) and bore the insignia of its unit — the winged angel of death — drawn by the American volunteer Stan Andrews, on the engine cowling.

HISPANO HA-1112 'BUCHON'

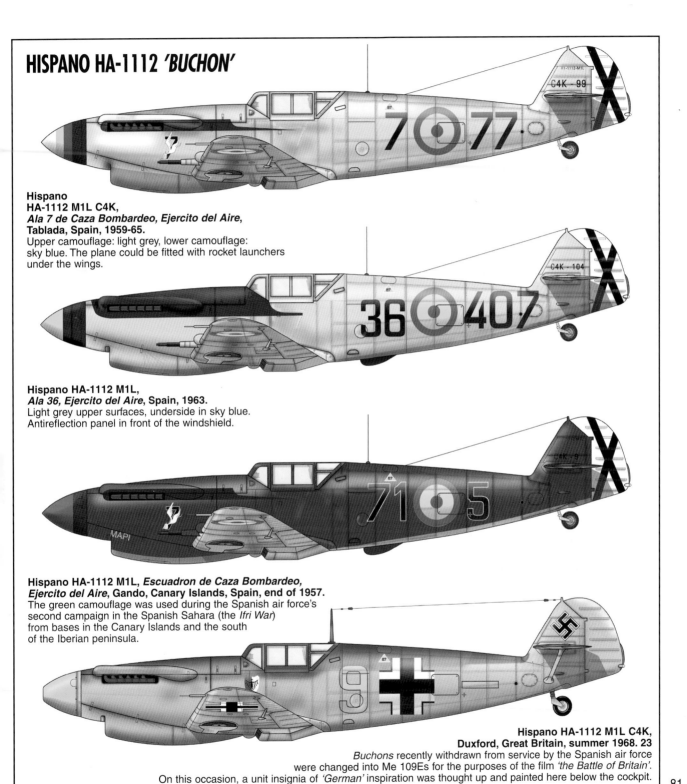

**Hispano
HA-1112 M1L C4K,
Ala 7 de Caza Bombardeo, Ejercito del Aire,
Tablada, Spain, 1959-65.**
Upper camouflage: light grey, lower camouflage:
sky blue. The plane could be fitted with rocket launchers
under the wings.

**Hispano HA-1112 M1L,
Ala 36, Ejercito del Aire, Spain, 1963.**
Light grey upper surfaces, underside in sky blue.
Antireflection panel in front of the windshield.

Hispano HA-1112 M1L, *Escuadron de Caza Bombardeo,
Ejercito del Aire*, **Gando, Canary Islands, Spain, end of 1957.**
The green camouflage was used during the Spanish air force's
second campaign in the Spanish Sahara (the *Ifri War*)
from bases in the Canary Islands and the south
of the Iberian peninsula.

**Hispano HA-1112 M1L C4K,
Duxford, Great Britain, summer 1968. 23**
Buchons recently withdrawn from service by the Spanish air force
were changed into Me 109Es for the purposes of the film *'the Battle of Britain'*.
On this occasion, a unit insignia of *'German'* inspiration was thought up and painted here below the cockpit.

81

BIBLIOGRAPHY

— **Luftwaffe code, marking and units**. H. Rosch. *Schiffer*
— **Les Messerschmitt espagnols**. *Hors série* n° 5, *Magazine Avions*.
— **Luftwaffe fighter aircraft in profile vol 1 et 2**. C. Sundin et C. Bergström. *Schiffer*.
— **Luftwaffe profiles n° 2: Bf 109 G/K**. M. Griehl. *Schiffer*
— **Bf 109 K camouflage and marking**. T. Poruba & K. Mil. *JAPO*
— **Bf 109 K**. *J. Ledwoch*. Militaria. Varsovie
— **Die Me 109 in Schweizer Flugwaffe**. G. Moch
— **Les Bf 109 roumains**. *Air Magazine* n°1
— **Luftwaffe emblems**. B. Ketley & M. Rolfe. *Hikoki*
— **Les Bf 109 finlandais**. Hors série n° 8, *Magazine Avions*
— **Bf 109 in Action**. *Squadron Signal* n° 57
— **Camouflage and marking vol n°1**. *Model Art*

— **Me 109 G/K**. *Flugzeug profil n°21*
— **Wings of Fame n°11**
— **JG 2 Richthofen**. *Osprey aviation* n° 1
— **JG 54 Grunherz**. *Osprey aviation* n° 6
— **Bf 109 on Western front**. J. Weal. *Osprey Aircraft* n°29
— **Bf 109 on Russian front**. J. Weal. *Osprey Aircraft* n°37
— **Bf 109 in North Africa**. J. Scutts. *Osprey Aircraft* n°2
— **Hungarian Air Force**. *Squadron Signal Publications*
— **Messerschmitt in action**. A. Ishoven & J. Cuny. *EPA*
— **Article sur le Bf 109 G**. V. Greciet in *WingMasters* n° 28
— **Bf 109 Slovaque**. Kudlica & M. Souffan. *Magazine Replic*
— **Bf 109 Bulgare**. Boshniakoc & C. Cony. *Magazine Avions* n°69
— **Les mulets de David**. Schlom Aloni. *Aéro journal* n° 22

AKNOWLEDGEMENTS

We should like to thank *Gérard Gorokhoff* and *Frédéric Lert* for their precious help during the realisation of this book

Design and Lay-out by André JOUINEAU and Yann-Erwin ROBERT, © *Histoire & Collections 2002 for the first print.*

Un ouvrage édité par
HISTOIRE & COLLECTIONS
SA au capital de 182 938, 82 €

5, avenue de la République
F-75541 Paris Cédex 11
Téléphone: 01 40 21 18 20
Fax: 01 47 00 51 11

This book has been designed, typed, laid-out and processed by *'Le studio graphique Armes & Collections'* fully integrated computer equipment.

Printed by ECGI
Spain, European Union
May 2004